The Irish and China

The Irish and China

ENCOUNTERS AND EXCHANGES

Edited by
Jerusha McCormack

NEW ISLAND

THE IRISH AND CHINA
First published in 2019 by
New Island Books
16 Priory Hall Office Park
Stillorgan
County Dublin
Republic of Ireland

www.newisland.ie

Hardback ISBN: 978-1-84840-720-6
Paperback ISBN: 978-1-84840-721-3
Epub ISBN: 978-1-84840-722-0
Mobi ISBN: 978-1-84840-723-7

Cover image: Dara Mac Donaill/ *The Irish Times*
Cover design: New Island Books
Index: Fergus Mulligan, www.publishing.ie
Typeset by JVR Creative India
Printed by TJ International Ltd, Padstow, Cornwall

This publication has received financial assistance from the Department of Foreign Affairs and Trade of Ireland.

New Island Books is a member of Publishing Ireland.

For David and Thomas
and John Blair
who also straddle worlds

Dear sons of Ireland,
the spirit of freedom will ever stand by you!
For you stand by one another,
you are the incarnation of freedom!

Guo Moruo, 'Victorious in Death' (1921)

Contents

UACHTARÁN NA hÉIREANN

PRESIDENT OF IRELAND

The first volume of *China and the Irish* appeared in 2009 as Ireland and China were marking the thirtieth anniversary of diplomatic relations. This present volume has been prepared to mark the fortieth anniversary, adding to the rich seam of experiences, connections and common endeavours which was brought to the public's attention in the first volume.

The chapters contained in this volume cover the full gamut of our common interests, be they the influence of Irish nationalism and literature on their Chinese counterparts, the similarities of Irish and Chinese philosophical thinking, the huge popularity of Irish dance and the growing popularity of Irish food in China, or the role of Irish botanists in discovering new Chinese plants, or that of Chinese astronomers in Ireland deepening our knowledge of the comets. They also reflect the deepening relationship between our two countries with interesting articles on the Chinese community in Ireland, the growth of Irish Studies in China and the growing importance of Irish food exports to China.

Since 2009, China has continued to develop at a very rapid rate and in many ways, China is a very different country today. It is now the second largest economy on the planet and its 1.4 billion people have attained unprecedented levels of prosperity and human development. China is becoming an increasingly important partner for Ireland and an increasingly important member of the international community. Increasingly sophisticated Chinese products and an increasing number of Chinese students and tourists are now to be seen across the island of Ireland.

I had the privilege of making a state visit to China in 2014 where I witnessed China's transformation at first hand. This year comes immediately after the fortieth anniversary of the opening up of the Chinese economy in 1978. That opening up has borne enormous benefits for China and its people. It is essential that we all of us now aim to deepen and strengthen multilateral approaches to the common problems we face, approaches that are built on universal values and solidarity across nations and peoples.

The editor of this book, Dr Jerusha McCormack, is to be complimented for her excellent stewardship of this volume as, indeed, of the first volume. Books such as this play no small part in ensuring that both of our peoples better understand our shared history. I wish the book every success.

MICHAEL D. HIGGINS
UACHTARÁN NA hÉIREANN
PRESIDENT OF IRELAND

Introduction

In the ten years since the publication of the first book of essays on Ireland/China relations, *China and the Irish*, Ireland has been transformed. Conventionally defined as a small open economy, it is now becoming an open and increasingly global culture. During the last decade, one which has commemorated the founding events of the Easter Rising of 1916, the notion of who is Irish must now be extended to include about two hundred nationalities. The country that once, over many centuries, said goodbye to its emigrating children is now saying hello to migrants from every corner of the world. Among these are the Chinese. As one of the essays in this new volume points out, the census of 2011 registered an increase of 91 per cent over the 2002 figure for Chinese migrants to Ireland. From a longer perspective, in just over half a century the Chinese in Ireland have changed from a largely 'unseen' small community into the fifth largest population of non-EU nationals in the country.

In turn, many Irish people now find themselves at home in China. In recent years, perhaps business people have seized the most visible lead in introducing Ireland to the larger People's Republic of China (PRC) public. As a result, Chinese consumers (as one essay points out) can, in their larger supermarkets, now routinely buy such products as Irish-based infant milk formula, Kerrygold butter, alcoholic beverages such as Bailey's Irish Cream and Jameson whiskey – and, even more recently, Irish beef and lamb. But, perhaps truer to its reputation, many Chinese people have already discovered Ireland through its culture – as represented by Irish writing and Irish dance. For almost a century now, as an essay tracking the emerging field of Irish Studies in China reports, Chinese readers have had the opportunity to become familiar

1

with the likes of G. B. Shaw, W. B. Yeats and Oscar Wilde. Fuelled in the last decades by translations of *Ulysses* and *Finnegans Wake*, that hunger for Irish writing is still growing. As embraced by their Chinese audience, Irish stories, told in peculiarly Irish ways, have opened the door for fresh perceptions of what, today, it means to be Irish.

These perceptions may perhaps be best summarized by the response to *Riverdance* – a theatrical show which, in 2019, is celebrating its twenty-fifth year by playing once again in the People's Republic of China. As editor, it astonishes me that the Chinese writers of two separate essays – one by the translator of *Finnegans Wake* and a second on *Riverdance* by two graduate students of ethnomusicology – essentially agree on what Ireland has come to mean for them and for its Chinese audience. As Dai Congrong, the translator of *Finnegans Wake*, relates, her first attraction to Joyce sprang from her sense that in his writing she was encountering Ireland's 'heart' – or what the Irish might call 'soul' – an emotional intelligence by which one perceives the world. Having read – and then translated – Joyce, Dai Congrong confesses that what she learned from Joyce was what it means to write 'from a heart that embraces this troubled world'. And that through his writing she found a new compassion for others, which she describes as 'sympathy' or, more simply, 'love'. Yet she also acknowledges that 'such a heart cannot survive in a highly hierarchical society'. Its exclusions, she finds, are alien to the kind of inclusivity she has discovered in Joyce and other Irish writing – one that, in embracing diversity, also embraces a new freedom.

By calling Joyce's *Finnegans Wake* 'the Book of Freedom', Dai also puts her finger on one of the qualities most cited by the two Chinese writers on *Riverdance*. Both remark at length on what they see as a new freedom of the audience to participate in the action – by stamping, clapping, even cheering or dancing in the aisles. That freedom is one that, like Dai's reading of Joyce, reaches out to embrace the audience by turning them from spectators into participants. It is that particular energy, as they register it, that allows *Riverdance* to incorporate such disparate elements as Spanish flamenco or Russian folk dance – without, as it were, skipping a beat. How does it do this? '*Riverdance*,' the writers observe, 'sought to reach people from all walks of life.' Or, in the words of Seamus Heaney (Ireland's latest winner of the Nobel Prize for Literature), its art involves us in enacting those rituals binding us into the 'human chain'. It is a perception of Irish solidarity crystallized by Guo Moruo in lines that serve as this book's epigraph: 'Dear sons of Ireland,' he exclaims: 'the spirit of freedom will ever stand by you! / For you stand by one another...'

In short, what these many essays testify to is the way that Irish culture – whether transported into Chinese homes by such media as the 2009 Chinese Central TV Spring Festival Gala broadcast or by translations of Irish events or Irish texts – has transformed its Chinese audience. Living within a quite rigidly defined hierarchical society, what has been the effect of these Irish interventions on the Chinese people? Have they served to remind them that, in common with the people of Ireland, they inhabit a republic: a nation constructed from the idea that the nation belongs to all its 'people'? What other parallels with Ireland do they invoke? As both the Republic of Ireland and the People's Republic of China can trace their evolution from Empire through colonization and modernization to their present contemporary status as wealthy and influential nations, China's warm embrace of Ireland's experience marks a singular transformation of one by the other – a transformation central to their mutual engagement, culturally, economically and politically.

Looking at other interventions of Irish events into recent Chinese history, this commonality between republics seems most pronounced in the political ferment which preceded their founding. One such moment is captured by Guo Moruo's revolutionary poem 'Victorious in Death', written on the occasion of the prolonged hunger strike staged by Irish Republican Terence MacSwiney in late 1920. While reading that poem, suddenly the myriad cultural distinctions between two nascent nations appear to be folded into a great translingual, transnational leap of solidarity, as the literary foreshadows the literal revolutions in both countries. Yet, as many of these essays demonstrate, such transformation is, in fact, mutual as well as ongoing. What has been changed, and changed utterly, in Ireland will in turn provoke change by what it has changed. It may well be said in future that the Chinese construction of Ireland through Joyce's writing or the performances of *Riverdance* could yet prove crucial for Ireland's own sense of itself: as proposing a vision of an Ireland that is open and equal, inclusive yet diverse, creative yet still in touch with its own traditions. For us who live here, it provides an image of an Ireland evolving into what, at its best, it might aspire to become: a vision in which we can find ourselves more truly – and more strange.

From the other side of the equation, it is important to register how China, translocated to Ireland, is also changing our understanding of our relations with the world outside. And not only to the outside world, but to the universe itself. In the work of Professor Tao Kiang, detailed in the memorial essay dedicated to his life, his move to Ireland, where he worked for decades as an astronomer at Dunsink Observatory, one discovers a model that is exemplary. Versed in classical Chinese literature, not only did Tao help initiate valuable professional links between China and Ireland, he also used his own knowledge of ancient Chinese astronomy to refine the Western understanding of the orbit, in one instance, of Halley's comet and its evolution over time. Kiang's concern for the larger picture is echoed in the essay by Joseph Grange, recalibrated by his former pupil Jim Behuniak, on the parallels between the philosophical principles of Daoism, one of China's native wisdom traditions, and those of perhaps Ireland's greatest thinker, John Scotus Eriugena. Another essay documents the translation of hitherto unknown Chinese plants to Ireland, leading to the transformation of our landscapes. Again, the story of the Columban Father Hugh MacMahon, relocated first to South Korea and then to China, reveals how his discovery of Confucian principles has sharpened his own vision of society as it is evolving in Ireland: finding in its traditions the same value placed on courtesy, flexibility and personal connections that he encountered during his work in China.

Translocation – whether actual or through one's imaginative engagement with the Other – results inevitably in transformation. In terms of this book: working on the first edition of *China and the Irish* ten years ago, I could find no Chinese writer to contribute to the volume. This time around, it was quite easy to find four – and even to discover others. Today more Chinese people in the PRC than ever know about Ireland, many of them in quite astonishing detail. More startling perhaps is the fact that more Chinese people than ever are choosing to settle in Ireland. Their sense of how their own identity has been challenged or transformed by this relocation reveals a diversity of response, depending on their place of origin, education and social class. But just as the Irish object to being lumped together as one and the same (usually according to stereotype) so do our new Chinese citizens, who quite rightly resist being designated simply as 'Chinese' – especially as a growing number of them are now actually born in Ireland. Addressing the other side of the equation, an Irishman who has worked both as an ecological consultant and now as an agent of Bord Bia (the Irish Food Board) details the difficulties and rewards of persuading the growing Chinese middle class that Irish food is 'good to eat'. In doing so, he has had to struggle to transform very different assumptions about the environment, its role in food production and diet. His is an exemplary tale of how one learns to honour difference of practice while simultaneously seeking to change attitudes towards one of the most basic necessities of our lives.

How can one straddle such different worlds? Every essay traces a new path – and that path, as the sage Zhuangzi once remarked, is made by the people walking it. Now reading through these essays, one is struck by how many of these new paths rest on a willing collaboration of spirit between the Irish and the Chinese. That this is an implicit, essential and ongoing spiritual collaboration seems clear from the correspondences between the vision of Daoism and that of the Christian teaching of John Scotus Eriugena. What the essay comparing them emphasizes, above all, is their shared conviction of the inherent, ineluctable connection of all phenomena. More concretely, that collaboration of spirit is evidenced in almost every essay of this book. It can be seen, for example, in the story of the Irish plant hunter Augustine Henry, whose work depended critically on his team of highly trained Chinese plant collectors – his best finds in Yunnan Province being attributed to the affectionately named 'Old Ho'. In cultural terms, such collaboration is evidenced everywhere in China by the achievements of the many intellectuals who have taken up the translation of key Irish texts – and/or are currently supporting the emerging field of Irish Studies in their own universities. It is striking, too, how many of these essays are written collaboratively – as well as the extent of the implicit cooperation on which I, as editor, depended on others for double-checking essays for accuracy as well as readability. Indeed, where would this book be without the trust with which my Chinese colleagues happily sent in their essays to be edited – or without my Irish collaborators who worked so long and hard to be exact in their assessment of how they saw Ireland's role in China or of the contributions of the many Chinese migrants to Ireland?

There is still a future before us. Both Ireland and China are changing rapidly, yet growing obviously closer both in understanding as well as through their many practical enterprises. To those ends this book is dedicated, in the expectation that, despite all difficulties of language or disparities of size and distance, both geographic and cultural, each will continue to learn from – and thereby continue to transform – the other during the decades to come.

Jerusha McCormack

An Irish Dao

JIM BEHUNIAK AND JOSEPH GRANGE

Apart from the fact that he was unmistakably Irish, little is known about the philosopher John Scotus Eriugena (c.810–c.880). He arrives mysteriously at the court of Charles the Bald in the middle of the ninth century. His outlook, without question, was formed somewhere other than the Frankish kingdom. John's mental landscape was one in which the taproot of an ancient Druid mysticism still mingled with the rich, learned traditions of Irish monasticism. He bore a name that was proudly redundant: John Scotus (the Irishman) Eriugena (born of Ireland). A learned and contemplative man, he had translated the arcane writings of mystical Greek philosophers into Latin. While in France, he set about formulating his own unique vision of God, Nature and divine creation – a work of remarkable scope and considerable heterodoxy – and one for which he was eventually condemned as a heretic and dismissed from the Frankish court. No one knows what became of John the Irishman after that.

Twelve centuries later the origin and destiny of the Cosmos that John pondered remains a mystery. Where did it come from? Where will it go? Many ages and cultures produce thinkers who, through the tools of human analysis, tackle such profound questions. Some succeed so well that their answers become dogmatic certainties that refuse to be questioned. Others fail so thoroughly that their questions become sceptical puzzles that refuse to be solved. Less frequently, but occasionally, there are thinkers who traverse the middle path between knowing and not knowing – thinkers for whom the tools of analysis bring understanding just to the edge of the unknown while preserving its mystery. From there, the thinker asks us, 'Do you see?' Analysis leaves off and realization begins. John was such a thinker – and so too was the fourth century BCE Daoist thinker, Laozi 老子.

If little is known about John the Irishman, even less is known about Laozi the Daoist. His name in Chinese means 'Old Master', which tells us exactly nothing. The text attributed to him is known as the Daodejing 道德經, the 'Classic of *Dao* and its Power'. The opening lines of the text offer a famous description of two aspects of the all-pervasive *Dao* 道 of things. There is 'named' *Dao* and 'unnamed' *Dao*. 'Named' *Dao* refers to the visible world with its colourful panorama of action, creation, decay and death, manifested in its recurrent cycles of becoming and perishing. As such, 'named' *Dao* represents everything that is 'here' (*you* 有) – the carousel of being in all its fullness, along with its inevitable companions: the good, the bad, the stable, the precarious. 'Unnamed' *Dao* refers to what is 'not here' (*wu* 無) – the primitive source of all things: the matrix of creativity that stands behind the flashing attractions of the world as we find it. What is this primitive source? Again, the Chinese word is *wu* 無, a word that means quite literally 'nothing'.

Thus, the opening chapter of the *Daodejing* observes two dimensions of world creation. It states: 'What is "nameless" is the origin of the heavens and the earth; and what is "named" is the mother of all things.' Alternately, the text allows us to read 'naming' (*ming* 名) as a verb, such that what is 'here' (*you* 有) designates the 'mother' of all things, whereas 'nothing' (*wu* 無) designates their 'beginnings'. In either case, the text is keen to relate that these are two sides of the same coin. What is 'here' and what is 'not here' work together in the complex process of creation. *Dao* is a name for the process itself – the ineluctable movement or flow whereby that which is 'not here' arrives and that which is 'here' gives way to its successors. In Daoist philosophy, this rhythmic cycle of change is marked by stops-and-starts that manifest different qualities as it moves. Thus it is 'Great', as in summer; 'Disappearing', as in autumn; 'Far-away', as in winter; and 'Returning', as in spring. In the perpetual beginnings-and-endings that mark out *Dao*-activity, we sense the presence of rhythm. John the Irishman will call this by its Latin name, *Natura*, or its Greek name, *Phusis*. He bore witness to its fourfold cadence in his own attempt to analyse that which resists such analysis.

John Scotus Eriugena's masterpiece is known by three titles drawn from three different languages. Its original title was the Greek phrase *Periphyseon*, which means 'About Nature'. Here the force of the Greek *Peri* yields a sense of ambient environing, as in the expression to walk around or about. It suggests an inquisitive, curious and thoughtful search after the meaning of Nature. And *Phusis*, in turn, bears with it a strong echo of its root source in the Greek word for 'Light'. Light and shadow play through Nature, and John is anxious that we sense the different qualities of transparency and darkness that abound in the world. What he is after is the 'felt sense' of the experience of Nature just as it is – its very 'suchness'.

This drive toward the 'suchness' of Nature loses some of its force when the Latin title is used: *De Divisione Naturae*. But if we remind ourselves that division is grounded in vision, then the force of the synonymous Greek term, *Theoria*, comes back into play as an act primarily associated with seeing the various planes, shapes and textures that express themselves throughout Nature. Finally, the English title, *On the Division of Nature*, seems very far away from the original connotations intended by John when he chose these words to speak about Nature and its creative processes. John, in fact, had a remarkably subtle idea of what he was doing with his own 'analysis'. The marking of divisions, of distinctions, was provisional. The aim was to 'see' one's way back from such divisions to the undivided whole from which they emerged. That is the very meaning of John's 'analytic' treatment. He explains:

> '*Analytike*' comes from the verb '*analuo*' which means 'I resolve' or 'I return'; for '*ana*' stands for 're-', '*luo*' for 'solve'. Thence comes also the noun 'analysis', which is similarly rendered 'resolution' or 'return' ... [Accordingly] '*Analytike*' is used in connection with the return of the division of the forms to the origin of that division.[1]

The most radical part of John's teaching is expressed in the very beginning of his work. He states that *Natura* includes everything: 'both the things which have and those which have not being'. Thus right away we are told 'that which is' and 'that which is not' will be the subject of investigation. In other words, what is 'here' (you 有) and what is 'not here' (wu 無) must find their place in this theory of everything. What is more, such an all-encompassing *Natura* takes pride of place even to the degree of pushing aside the term 'God' in John's writings. One cannot overestimate the radical boldness of speculation mirrored here in John's deliberately selected vocabulary. Like all great thinkers, he aims to shock his readers out of their ordinary and routine thoughts at the very beginning of his *magnum opus* – and that he certainly did.

There is good reason, however, that 'God' yields to *Natura* in John's analysis. 'God' cannot be approached through analysis, but only in the reversal of analysis through the resolution of *Analytike*. This is where analysis leaves off and realization begins. For John, this is the 'returning' dimension of his understanding of Nature. It is this 'nameless' aspect that requires John to speak of the *Deus Absconditus*, the 'Hidden God' that can never yield to affirmative expression. It is John's contention that speaking and knowing are not the same. There are ways of knowing the hidden dimension of Nature that do not involve speaking. In this way of thinking, he agrees with the *Daodejing* that teaches in its fifty-sixth chapter: 'Those who know do not speak, and those who speak do not know.'

John's analysis of the 'Division of Nature' involves four planes or levels. However, given his 'analytic' method, it is important to understand that his 'divisions' are not merely theoretical distinctions; they are rather ways or aspects of experiencing Nature. As we shall soon see, these 'divisions' flow into each other by reason of a radically new understanding of causality that John borrows from the Eastern Orthodox Fathers. The dimensions of Nature here examined are really perspectives that yield up from their own angle of vision different expressions of Nature as it flows forth from creation and then finds its 'return' to that original source. Like any perspective, each of these four ways of understanding Nature has its own special manifestation that stresses one aspect of reality. Each therefore tends to light up one region and shade another. For John, it is the interplay between them that grants us a whole and unified portrait of Nature. His four-fold

Natura is thus a holistic matrix within which genuine 'manifestations' of divinity appear from four distinct perspectives. These *theophanies* (or 'divine manifestations') are not always 'known' or 'speakable', although they can be felt and experienced. John's philosophy tries to help us acquire the power to take such a leap into the realm of felt experience.

Turning to the actual text of the *Periphyseon*, we find John's 'Division of Nature' unfolding into a four-way process of 'emergence', 'expression', 'manifestation' and 'return' to the nameless creative source. The divisions, respectively, are as follows:

> The *first* division is the division into what creates and is not created.
> The *second* into what is created and creates.
> The *third* into what is created and does not create.
> The *fourth* into what is not created and does not create.[2]

The Alpha, origin, or source of all *theophanies* is Nature on the first level – that which creates and is not created. This beginning is the God of Christian religion and philosophy and, again, it is significant that John includes this infinite presence of power in Nature itself. The act of coming to presence (what the Chinese call *you* 有) seems more important to John than any of the other divine attributes. True enough, he provides quite orthodox divine attributes later on in his *Periphyseon* – but as noted earlier, this unification of Nature and creative emergence is an extremely bold speculative move given his time and culture. We shall soon see how this deference to Nature and creativity rises out of his roots in ancient Irish and very early Christian Greek culture.

The first level is bookended by the fourth level: the Nature that neither creates nor is created. Its place in the scheme of Nature is necessary to complete Nature's systematic unity. Just as there is a beginning, which pours forth creative power so that what is 'here' (*you* 有) enters into other perspectives of Nature, so also there is a 'return' whereby light, life and power return to their source in what is 'not here' (*wu* 無). This theme of the 'return' is also to be seen in the *Daodejing*, where that which comes into being 'moves back' (*fan* 反) into the shadows of presence and yields its space to what is forthcoming.

Here, the mysteries of creation and the 'nameless' *Dao* take on their most cloaked presence. The cycle of presence–absence repeats itself through all of Nature's *theophanies*. For John, this journey forth from, and back to, whence all things came has its Christian affirmation in the concepts of resurrection and salvation. But even here there is a tinge of difference in his thinking: the return is not simply a matter of personal salvation but rather a process of 'deification' whereby we become absorbed in the absent presence of Creation itself. The creator (God or *Dao*) is a creative movement, not a static 'Being' (*Esse*) that 'creates'. It is a *process*, not a substance or a thing. The structure of its journey is the perfect circle that repeats itself again and again but is never exhausted. From within the second and third divisions of Nature, this abstract process is felt and experienced in ever-novel ways.

The second perspective on Nature grants a vision of that which is created and creates. It is closely allied to the third level and, in fact, just as John reduces perspectives one and four to a synthesis, he also unites levels two and three such that each item that is 'here' (*you* 有) can be simultaneously viewed as *creator* and *created* within the matrix of world creation – much like parents are both progenies and progenitors in their lines of transmission. It is at the second and third levels, however, that conventional commentators often err in their understanding of John. Having recourse to the strictest interpretations of Neoplatonic philosophy, the 'created' is taken to be a static, unchanging realm of ideas (*eidos*) that swings free from the vicissitudes of creative emergence. By couching the second and third divisions within the framework of the first and fourth divisions, however, John means to affirm the dynamism of the dual, creative/created aspect of things that come to be in the second and third divisions. Modern readers quite rightly refuse to entertain a realm of invisible ideas that exist solely by themselves in eternal perfection. Thus, it is precisely here that we ask the reader to cast aside (for the remainder of this essay) any such conventional interpretation of medieval Platonism. For we believe that John's insights were different – they were ahead of their time.

Again, the customary explanation of the second division – that which is created and creates – is that it is a dimension filled with Platonic ideas (*eidos*) of which the creatures of sensible nature are only mere copies. These ideas are 'made' by God through the activity of the divine mind and they are the means by which the second and third levels come to presence. The principal fallacy in this interpretation is that it involves an incorrect interpretation of causation. Western philosophers tend to overstress Aristotle's distinctions between 'material' and 'efficient' causation. The 'material' cause, for Aristotle, is the *material* that accounts for the appearance of something (e.g. the marble that makes the sculpture), whereas the 'efficient' cause is the *action* that accounts for the appearance of something (e.g. the sculptor who makes the sculpture). It is natural enough, one supposes, to see the world creator as a 'maker' of some kind. But when that leads to a search for some kind of 'material' from which the world is made, then a confused conflation of 'material' and 'efficient' causality has occurred. Platonic ideas (*eidos*) become, for some thinkers, like material things that are taken up in the act of 'creation', which is then modelled on some form of 'efficient' causation. But the genuine Platonic understanding of causality is quite different from that of a 'maker' who stands outside the creative act. Rather, the creator is *within* all the levels of the creative process. Thus, John properly calls things in the world – foxes, trees, ice, fire and water, among other things – *theophanies*. They utter forth (*phon*) the presence of the creator (*Theos*). John is quite clear about this. Their origin is not in *some-thing* but in *no-thing*. 'The word "nothing" here,' writes John, 'does not refer to some kind of material, or even to some kind of cause.'[3]

John thus appeals not to an Aristotelian reading of causality, but rather to a purely Platonic theory handed down by the early Christian Greek Fathers. In this theory, the creator is a continuing *presence* within the effect.

Another way to understand this causal thinking is by concentrating on the term 'influence'. The etymology of this term provides a very concrete image of the kind of causal efficacy that John has in mind. *In-fluere* in Latin means 'to flow into'. It is therefore a continuing process. Unlike 'efficient' causation, which when it is done stands apart and outside from its effect, influence continues *into* the operations of the process of which it is part. It is as much a part of the effect as it is of the cause. Influence is *internally* related to its effect.

This internal character stands in stark contrast to other sorts of causation, which are entirely external to the effects they seek to bring about. An influence *stays* with its object for as long as that object manifests its power of expression.

Thus, in the forehead of a primate we can see the influence of a brain that will later help shape our own cranial capacities. The causal efficacy exhibited through such *theophanies* is one in which causes and effects crisscross and entwine with each other (such that in the second and third divisions each thing is both 'creator' and 'created'). As such, there is a thick net of influences penetrating Nature's web of relations. So dense are these connections that there are even times when the effect can exceed its cause and actually *evolve* into something brand new. This is a doctrine no strictly Aristotelian or Scholastic philosopher could maintain. But in John's universe, it can become a quite regular event because of the mutual play of influences thriving in Nature. He was thus on Darwin's side.

When looking at Nature through the perspectives of the second and third divisions, one cannot help but observe its outstanding creative power. From beginning to end, from Alpha to Omega, from 'named' to 'nameless' *Dao* 道, we experience Nature as a passage into novelty; it boils over with the presence of creativity. Through this unrest we catch a glimpse of creation's way. The first and fourth perspectives alert us to the contingency and sheer wonder of things. The second and third perspectives alert us to the created world as it drives towards fulfilling the divine influence resident in each creaturely manifestation. The view granted us by the second level is one that shines with the creative power of God when it is structured toward bringing into presence specific potential influences – possibilities that can be realized as they carry over into future events. This is why John speaks of the second division in terms of *prototypia, exemplars, paradeigmata, theoriae, volitiones, participationes* and *fundamenta*. In using such terms (and many others throughout the *Periphyseon*) he is providing his contemporaries with the greatest possible synthesis of the then-available philosophical systems. Among his sources are Plato, Plotinus, the Stoics, Augustine and the early Greek Fathers. Since each of these thinkers relied on a host of other thinkers, we can rightly say that John was summing up the best philosophy available at that time; it represents in effect a veritable Summa of philosophic sources then at hand.

Enabling John's peculiar genius was his inclination and willingness to approach Nature itself as divine process, thus building upon a Celtic sensibility that predates the Christian idiom in which he worked. It is the profound respect for Nature in all her manifestations that leads to John's choice of 'Nature' as the term best suited to express the sweep of reality's compass – a totality that he does not hesitate to call *To Hen*, 'the One' that encompasses the many. This choice requires that he use the feminine possessive pronoun when speaking of God. Hence, in the first and fourth perspectives, readers were sometimes shocked to hear John occasionally refer to 'she' or 'her' when speaking of God and Nature. But John never hesitates, nor does he apologize for such usages. When the divine process is envisioned as one that does not stand back from creation but verily *gives birth* and *nourishes* the growth of its offspring, the feminine imagery recommends itself to imagination. In the opening chapter of the *Daodejing*, Laozi speaks of 'named' *Dao* as the 'mother' (*mu* 母) of things – the ever-present (*you* 有) source of influences that shape, support and sustain our being. Meanwhile, the 'unnamed' *Dao* is portrayed in Chapter Six as the 'mysterious female' or 'dark womb' (*xuanpin* 玄牝) from which all things spring.

John's acute sensitivity to such things was steeped in the Irish sense of the spectacular nearness of Nature that surrounds us at all places and times. The novel meaning of causality in John's system can be further understood through an examination of the process of 'participation'. Participation theory originates with Plato and his attempt to join the worlds of permanence and change, being and becoming. To take part in something is to let that power manifest itself throughout one's own nature. It is therefore primarily a way in which the cause stays active and alive within the effect. A thorough theory of participation such as John's would entail myriad lines of causation branching out and through Nature so as to connect the different levels. Furthermore, since these participations are also *theophanies*, it means that God's presence is everywhere, though in different shades and degrees. This fact proves that John's system is not the same as the strict hierarchical structure that the Neoplatonic philosophers insisted on. Rather, it is much looser, with horizontal as well as vertical influences causing novelty to emerge

15

at unexpected times in unexpected places to unsuspecting subjects. In the presence of such divine influences, humans find their place in John's *Natura*. We participate alongside other *theophanies* as extensions of God's influence; and through effort and grace, we actually come to manifest the divine process.

Such experience is not the domain of mystics alone. Every human being has the capacity to live and to contribute within the second and third divisions. In fact, it is in taking up such a participatory stance in the middle of the creative process that we can sense the 'natural' way to live. Here also, we believe, is the place where Daoist consciousness resides. The Daoist has a different way of describing such participation – namely, 'spontaneity' (*ziran* 自然), whereby things join in the process of *Dao* by realizing their natures alongside the myriad things – bamboo, water, stones and plain food – the ordinary *theophanies* of Dao. However, it is plain to see that John's speculative system leaves room for mystical experiences akin to those that Daoism affords.

To approach such experiences, it is wise to recall a summary of the whole of John's vision. John J. O'Meara provides an excellent one:

> [To] recapitulate the whole work – we have divided Nature, which comprises God and his creatures, into four parts. The *first* consists of the Nature which creates and is not created (God as Beginning); the *second* of the Nature which is created and creates (the primordial causes); the *third* of the Nature which is created and does not create (the effects – mainly sensible nature); the *fourth* of that which neither is created nor creates (God as End).[4]

In the synthesis of all four perspectives, God is envisioned beginning to end – not as a 'Being' (*Ens*) but as the ongoing process of both creating and being created.

This is perhaps where John's system is most strikingly congruent with Daoist thinking. The term '*Dao*' is itself a process term. The character (道) consists of two parts. At its centre is an eye (目) and a forehead that sees *forward*, while behind and beneath it is the 'movement' or 'going' radical (辶) which indicates running along. In a strikingly similar vein, John provides an extraordinarily provocative definition of

God early in the *Periphyseon*. He does so by examining the word 'God' (*Theos*) itself. John writes:

> Etymologically, the name is from the Greek. Either it derives from the verb *theoreo* (i.e. I see) or *theo* (i.e. I run), or more probably from both, since they contain one and the same meaning. For when *theos* [God] is derived from the verb *theoreo*, it is regarded as seeing. For it sees in itself all that exists because it sees nothing outside of itself, since nothing is outside of it. When *theos* is derived from the verb *theo*, *theos* [God] is justly understood as *running*, for it flows through all things and is in no sense stagnant, but fills all things – moving through them.[5]

An extraordinary expression! God as a 'runner'. It brings together every aspect of John's vision: from the unification of his four 'divisions' to his unique approach to 'causality'; i.e. the running influence (or *influere*) of all things into their successors.

From within this creative process, we see most clearly from the second and third perspectives what is immediately 'here' (*you* 有). Our vision of the whole is not complete, however, without apprehending the mysterious source that is 'not here' (*wu* 無) – that distance from which the creative process has come and the not-yet future towards which it leads. Along with God, we 'run' our course from beginning to end only to 'return' to from where we came. The 'nameless' *Dao* in this respect is shrouded in obscurity. Its echoes, however, are certainly to be found within the ancient Irish theory of the 'Three Circles' (*triquetra*) of cyclical power: Birth, Death and Rebirth – and, of course, it is a central theme in various forms throughout Asiatic thought. So whether we are talking about rebirth, resurrection, reincarnation or transmigration, creative transformation is a pivotal theme in a wide segment of philosophical and religious thinking.

What John means by 'return' is indicated in the phrase that he used earlier, 'deification'. This way of thinking about human destiny is to be found in a highly articulated form in the writings of the early Greek Fathers. So it is within the writings of the Pseudo-Dionysius, Maximus the Confessor and Gregory of Nyssa that the meaning of creative

17

transformation is grounded. Its primary meaning is that the human being is meant to become more and more God-like in his or her travels through the temporal realm. This process is very similar to the kind of consciousness-raising that is part of Buddhist and Daoist practice. It is also similar to the transformations undergone by the devotees of yoga or meditation as they try to transform the energy in the body into more and more refined states. Yet what is most distinctive about the Greek Eastern Orthodox understanding is the way in which this process culminates in the assimilation of the creature into the divine nature. This is quite different from the Latin Western understanding of salvation as confined to the individual soul with all its personal qualities transformed to a higher state. The West emphasizes the importance of the *individual* soul – and even to this day, Western Christianity has a tinge of selfishness associated with its doctrine of redemption. Such selfishness is utterly absent both in the work of John Scotus Eriugena and in the *Daodejing*.

Thus, despite their many differences, John and Laozi remain our steadfast friends as we ponder the same mysterious cosmos that they pondered. Rather than assert dogmatic certainties or generate sceptical puzzles, each thinker uses the tools of human analysis to the extent possible – pointing out different dimensions of the world so that we might provisionally 'see' such things. Once such divisions are glimpsed, each thinker urges us to complete the *Analytike* by restoring such distinctions to their deeper level of unity – thereby returning ourselves to the pre-theoretical flow. John's analysis of *Natura* begins with a vision of 'both the things which *have* and those which *have not* being'. Similarly, the *Daodejing* begins with what is 'here' (*you* 有) and what is 'not here' (*wu* 無). As the same Daoist passage reminds us, however, 'these two flow from the same source, though differently named. And both are regarded as dark obscurities. From obscurity to deeper obscurity, this is the door to the profoundest mysteries' – and so too for John, the divisions of Nature conceal something 'divine and ineffable', the 'inscrutable secret, the invisible, incomprehensible, profound mystery!'[6] John and Laozi remind us that such mysteries transcend both our individual cultures and our individual selves, such that we all 'run' together from beginning-to-end.

Endnotes

1   Johannes Scotus Eriugena (2006), *Periphyseon*, trans. I.P. Sheldon-Williams, in *Basic Issues in Medieval Philosophy: Selected Readings*, eds. Richard N. Bosley and Martin Tweedale, Peterborough, Canada: Broadview Press, p. 611.

2   Johannes Scotus Eriugena (1976), *Periphyseon*, trans. Myra L. Uhlfelder, Indianapolis: The Bobbs Merrill Company, p. 2.

3   Johannes Scotus Eriugena (1969), *Periphyseon*, trans. A.B. Wolter, in *Medieval Philosophy: From St. Augustine to Nicholas of Cusa*, eds. Paul Edwards and Richard H. Popkin, New York: The Free Press, p. 133.

4   John J. O'Meara (1988), *Eriugena*, Oxford: Clarendon Press, p. 153.

5   *Eriugena*, 1969, p. 131.

6   Ibid.

In the Footsteps of James of Ireland: Encounters with Irish Missionaries in China

Hugh MacMahon

It will come as a surprise to many that the first recorded Irishman to visit China was a certain mysterious James of Ireland. A Franciscan friar, he accompanied his Italian confrere, Odoric of Pordenone, on his epic travels across the globe between 1318 and 1330, some fifty years after the more famous voyage of Marco Polo.

James joined Odoric at Ormus in India, from whence they journeyed together by sea to Sumatra and Borneo and then on to Guangzhou in China. There Odoric and James spent the years 1323–8 travelling and preaching all over the country, including three years in Beijing at the court of the Great Khan, where they were probably attached to the church presided over by the ageing Franciscan Archbishop Montecorvino. After returning to Italy (over the land route, through central Asia), Odoric related a chronicle of their travels shortly before he died. This became as popular in its time as the account of Marco Polo, although its reputation suffered through the sloppily plagiarized version of Sir John Mandeville. But the only further mention of James was in 1331, when the good citizens of Udine, Odoric's home town, awarded James two Marks for accompanying their illustrious hero on his adventures.

Much of Odoric's account relates to the marvels they saw or heard about during their travels. Many of these are eyewitness accounts of the customs of the Chinese people, such as his descriptions of the practice of fishing with tame cormorants, of the habit of letting the fingernails grow extravagantly and of the practice of foot-binding. But some instances are literally incredible, as when they were told by their hosts of a region in which ripe melons burst open to reveal a small animal like a lamb – giving the people both melon and meat. James, apparently not to be outdone, responded that in Ireland there were trees that produce birds!

Beyond this we know little of what James shared with those he met or how he was changed by the experience. It was not until five hundred years later, in the early to mid-nineteenth century, that Christian missionaries – Presbyterians, Anglicans, Methodists and Catholics – followed in James's footsteps to China. There they lived through eventful times, having to cope with Japanese invasions and civil wars, as well as those natural disasters that dogged China's opening to the West from the early 1800s. Eventually all left or were expelled by 1954 under the revolutionary Communist government.

A long forty years later, when China opened again to the wider world, I had the opportunity to discover something of the impression those Irish missionaries had made and the challenges that had faced them. I had been appointed to Hong Kong as manager of a non-government organization sending volunteers to teach in mainland universities. As a result, I had the opportunity to visit many of the major cities across this vast country. But first I was to spend five months in Wuhan learning Mandarin. Although progress in the language proved slow, it was an ideal place to start searching for traces of former Irish missionaries' involvement in China.

Wuhan: Disasters and Scholars

Wuhan is a river city. Although 600 nautical miles up the Yangtze River from the sea, it still remains accessible to ocean-going vessels. Today, with a population of over ten million, Wuhan is the largest city in central China; or, more accurately, Wuhan is a collective of three sister cities – Wuchang, Hankou and Hanyang – each divided from the other by the Yangtze and a tributary, the Han. Wuchang is the ancient provincial city on the south-east bank; directly across the Yangtze is Hanyang, the industrial town. Below Hanyang, and divided from it by the Han River, is Hankou with its historic foreign concession.

Historically, the two rivers made Wuhan a transport and commercial hub; but their flooding also led to regular disasters. In 1931 an exceptional flood caused the deaths of 150,000 people. Dark lines high on the side of a bank building in Hankou still bear witness to the height the waters reached that year. After the drownings came typhoid and cholera, followed by measles and smallpox.

At that time there were two Irish groups in Wuhan that responded immediately to the crisis. In Hankou, Irish Methodist missionaries, including Dr Sally Wolfe from Skibbereen, County Cork, operated hospitals that escaped the floods but were soon swamped with people. Across the river in Hanyang, the Irish Columban Fathers had to abandon their flooded rural parishes to join other refugees in the city. Though the religious society was founded only thirteen years previously, they already had sixty-four priests in China, forty of them in the Hanyang area. Their leader, Bishop Edward Galvin, reported, 'All around the mission is that helpless, starving multitude. In all my years in China [at this point, fifteen] I have never seen such a terrible sight. From the hill at the rear of our residence the entire countryside, as far as the eye can reach, is one vast sea of water. We can do little to alleviate the sufferings but we are doing our best.' At the time, the residence itself was under fifteen feet of water; only the upper floor could be used. From there the Columbans organized relief operations. Meanwhile, the Columban Sisters, having just completed a convent nearby, handed it over to 436 women and children. To add to the confusion, bandits were raiding the almost deserted villages by boat and had kidnapped a priest, Fr Hugh Sands – an occurrence that was becoming alarmingly familiar.

In 1938 another major disaster struck. In August floods again broke the embankments on the river. On top of that, the Japanese army, advancing slowly across China, began launching daily bombing raids on all three cities. When it became obvious that eighty-five thousand refugees were about to descend on Wuhan, Bishop Galvin was appointed chair of the Wuhan Refugee Zone Committee and began organizing food and shelter for flood victims and war refugees. To better coordinate the work, he moved over to Hankou where he was welcomed to stay in the Methodist hospital. When the Japanese army finally entered Hankou, ordering seventy thousand refugees to leave for camps outside the walls, Bishop Galvin organized and led the exodus. According to one eyewitness, when the bishop saw a crippled boy hobbling along, he 'took him on his broad shoulders and carried him safely along the sorrowful trail and down through the densely crowded streets of Hankou'.

Witnessing all these events was Dr Sally Wolfe. Since she had arrived in China in 1915, she had worked tirelessly to serve the sick and injured, regardless of race or religion. During the Japanese occupation, she was in the nearby city of Chungsiang, where she succeeded in keeping Japanese soldiers out of the hospital there. Earlier she had adopted three Chinese infants, a boy and two girls. When she finally left China in 1951 they were in their mid to late twenties. She was never to hear from them again. On her departure from Hankou the hospital staff presented her with two scrolls, one of which said, 'Her name is known throughout China and foreign countries and her virtue enriches gold.' She returned to Cork, dying there in 1975 at the age of ninety. Today her work is commemorated in a book called, appropriately, *She Left Her Heart in China: The Story of Dr. Sally Wolfe, Medical Missionary 1915– 1951*. Bishop Galvin was in turn expelled in September 1952, charged with 'opposing and obstructing the establishment of an Independent Church in China'.

When I arrived in Wuhan in 1995, the building that the Columbans occupied was still there, in use as a middle school. Bishop Galvin's tiny house has also survived behind the modest cathedral that he had built in Hanyang. And people in the countryside began enquiring when the Irish priests and sisters they had known would be coming to visit them once again.

However, the Wuhan I knew in 1995 already belonged to a different era. It was beginning to modernize, even though traces of the old socialist work-unit system – by which people worked, lived, shopped, studied and received medical treatment all in one location – still survived. I studied at Hubei University in Wuchang, in a class of two students. The teacher was a retired professor who believed in the traditional method of having the student learn off a page of text each day. My fellow student was a young man from Queensland University, and each afternoon he opted for traditional painting and martial arts, leaving me alone with the rather severe and formidable professor. He had little English and, as my stock of Chinese words was limited, I resorted to my knowledge of Korean and a Korean dictionary in which each word was accompanied by its Chinese equivalent.

During these sessions I asked him about traditional expressions and traditions, based on the Confucianism I had come to know in Korea. He replied that when he was young such customs existed but they had been discontinued in the Mao era. His interest deepened when I told him that Korea had managed to preserve its Confucian spirit, not only in its ancient Sungkyunkwan University but also in the people's everyday language and habits. Ironically, perhaps, until 1906 Wuchang had been one of the provincial centres where young men sat those critical Imperial exams in Confucian learning on which a place in the civil service, and thus the family fortunes, would depend. The professor himself, though he was probably not conscious of it, was a product of that tradition. And as I quickly realized, he offered a good example of how Confucianism still survived in China, its homeland. For the Confucian gentleman or *junzi* is formal, is careful in his language lest he offend, and runs his family and/or business by the weight of respect that his self-control and dignity commands. He does this because he has been brought up to believe that, by developing 'sageliness within and kingliness without', his mind, his family and his country will each find peace and harmony to the benefit of all.

Coming from self-asserting Europe, I was surprised to discover that, in fact, the West does not have a monopoly on individualism. Chinese society is also centred on developing the individual spirit – but from a different viewpoint. There, traditionally, personal self-interest takes second place to social responsibility. To find meaning in life as well as to succeed in the world, one must first come to know and rule one's self. This self-discipline and readiness to learn from others finds expression in the *junzi* – a person daily seeking a deeper understanding of themselves and the world around them. In the West this self-control and downplaying of the ego may seem restrictive; but in China it was – and still is – recognized as the first step in civilizing humans.

Not that the Chinese have ever been unaware of the attractions of personal wealth. The first story in the *Book of Mencius*, Confucius' most famous follower, is about Mencius' visit to the court of the king of Liang. The king asked the scholar, 'How can your teaching profit my state?' Mencius replied that if the king asks, 'How can I profit my state?' the ministers will ask, 'How can we profit our estates?' and the nobles and commoners will ask, 'How can we profit ourselves?' Thus individuals would compete with each other for profit and all would suffer as a result. Mencius concluded, 'I have come to teach the good relationships (*Ren*) and social duties (*Yi*) of Confucius. If these flourish the king and all his people will prosper. Please do not speak of profit.' Elsewhere Confucius said, 'From the ruler down to the common people, all must consider the cultivation of the person as the root of everything else.'

Such an attitude came naturally to my Wuhan professor, though he was probably unaware of the impression it made on Westerners. It struck me that Bishop Edward Galvin would have recognized in people like the professor a dignity, humility and respect for learning that he would have known among older folk back in Ireland. Nor is the Chinese tendency to use polite words to avoid direct confrontation and to express their wishes indirectly unknown in the Irish tradition. Deference to others and the common good was certainly embedded in both traditions; but the Confucians had institutionalized it through ritual, education and family life to a degree that still astonishes Westerners.

Changchun: Laws and Relationships

Three hours' flight from Wuhan to the cold north of China is the modern city of Changchun. Once the capital of the Japanese puppet state of Manchuria, it was briefly headed by the 'Last Emperor', Pu Yi, whose unimposing palace survives. It is also famous as the centre of Chinese film production and the cradle of China's automobile industry.

As a provincial capital, it has over twenty-seven universities; and since our teachers were at least six of them, I visited there often.

One of these teachers was an Australian lawyer who lectured at Jilin University. One cold winter night there, over a glass or two of his favourite cherry brandy, he described his work there, explaining to his students the differences between civil law and common law. Civil law, of Roman origins, is based on codes of law and is the basic system in China. Common law comes from the British tradition and is based on precedent. It has been adopted in many other parts of the world and so also forms part of the Chinese curriculum. When his explanations wound down, I asked him if any efforts were being made to preserve the traditional Chinese attitude to law. He asked me to explain. I quoted Confucius, 'Govern the people by laws and regulate them by penalties and they will try to do no wrong but they will lose the sense of shame. Govern the people by virtue and restrain them by rules of propriety and the people will have a sense of shame and be reformed by themselves!'

By way of contrast, the Qin Emperor (who built the Great Wall) used strict laws and regulations to unify the country, thus starting a debate between the Legalist School and traditional Confucianists. The Legalists viewed human nature as weak and thus in need of severe laws and harsh penalties to control its impulses. Mainstream Confucianists, however, believed in the basic goodness of people, holding that they just needed to be educated to bring out the best in them. Fortunately, the disciples of Confucius prevailed, and the emphasis on educating people to play their role in society responsibly continued for another two thousand years. I believe that this type of education is the real reason Chinese culture remains so strong and distinctive throughout all of East Asia.

At the heart of such an education is the development, from a young age, of a sense of mutually responsible relationships between parents and children, husband and wife, between siblings, between friends and between subject and ruler. A famous example of this thinking is the discussion reported between Confucius and the Duke of Sheh, who, when visiting, boasted, 'Among us there are those who may be styled upright in their conduct: if their father stole a sheep they would bear witness to the fact.' Confucius, quite horrified, replies, 'In our part of the country those who are upright are different. The father conceals the misconduct of the son and the son conceals the misconduct of the father. Uprightness is to be found in this.' This difference of perspective continues to spark debates today, so that even a thousand years later a leading Neo-Confucian scholar, Chao Chi, could reaffirm, 'A son may lie to conceal his father's stealing.'

As a practising lawyer, my Australian colleague saw difficulties in implementing this approach in a world where commerce demands safeguards with no exceptions. However, it is in the commercial field that the survival of the old attitude still remains noticeable. Western businessmen experience its implications when it comes to making contracts. In China a written agreement, no matter how well drafted or witnessed, can just be a piece of paper. The economic situation may change or there might be temporary setbacks, so written words can lose their relevance. What makes business work is the relationship in terms of the resulting trust built up between the two parties. That is what overcomes difficulties and sees the project through.

In fact, it was in Changchun that the eminent Irish Presbyterian missionary Andrew Weir faced exactly into this tension between written law and human circumstance. Towards the end of his first term in Manchuria (1900–8), he began to question whether all the laws of the Church were of equal importance and set in concrete. The situation in north China was clearly different from that back home. For instance, it was next to impossible for people to observe a strict Sabbath. Given this situation, Andrew Weir believed that the spirit of the message was more important than rules and regulations, saying of the law, 'Do not bind it as a fetter on men.' It should be sufficient that a person agrees with the essential doctrines of the Westminster Confession. This Confucian-like ability to apply humane considerations and seek solutions led to his playing a key role in the development of the Presbyterian Church in Manchuria.

Andrew Weir had first arrived in Manchuria from Cookstown in County Tyrone in 1900, just in time to experience the trauma of the anti-foreigner Boxer Uprising. Worse, the missionaries' efforts to provide medical and educational services while spreading the gospel were to be continuously disrupted by banditry, World War I, the Japanese occupation, unequal relations with the Western powers as well as the growing pains of a newly independent China. As clerk of the Presbyterian Synod for twenty-seven years, Weir was determined to persevere in his efforts to make the Manchurian Church self-governing, self-supporting and self-evangelizing. By the time he died from typhus in Changchun in 1933, those goals had been largely achieved. His son, Jack, who was born in Changchun, later became a highly respected voice in the peace process in Northern Ireland as Moderator of the Presbyterian Church. In this role, he displayed much of his father's openness and perseverance in seeking practical solutions to intractable problems. That skill in finding pragmatic solutions to apparently insoluble conflicts of value or principle may well have been a lesson learned from his father's role in China.

Today an imposing church, accommodating six thousand and 'built in an Irish Protestant church style', stands in the middle of Changchun. Built originally by English Presbyterians in 1897, it was taken over by the government-run Three-Self Patriotic Christian Church [the official face of Christianity in the PRC] in 1959. In 1998 the present church was constructed on the site; beside it stands Changchun Women's Hospital, originally run by Irish Presbyterians. As Andrew Weir's base for most of his life in Manchuria, these two institutions testify to his legacy and, over the decades, to that of many other Irish missionaries.

Fuzhou: Chinese Science and Western Education

Fuzhou, the coastal capital of Fujian province, was one of my favourite places to visit. At that time I was unaware that Odoric and James had walked its streets almost seven hundred years earlier, finding it 'a mighty fine city, standing upon the sea'.

The schools at which we had teachers were located on Nantai, once an island in the Min River but now joined to its southern bank across from the old city. It was there that a foreign concession was built in 1844: a little enclave of Western consulates, churches and schools on and around a modest hill. Today the remains of these semi-abandoned buildings can be explored (if you are willing to climb through the narrow alleys) – though as plans are afoot to modernize the area, these relics of another age may not survive long.

The reason foreigners were originally segregated in this area across the river was because the locals did not want them in their cities. As there was an old graveyard on Nantai – said to be haunted – no Chinese would live there. And if the ghosts haunted the Westerners, all the better. It was only in later years that Westerners began to understand this Chinese attitude to ghosts. Since ancient times in China it was believed that a person had at least two souls. There is the material or bodily soul (*gui*), which leaves the body at death – but remains near the grave or place of death for three or more years. These are the 'ghosts' that could haunt an island like Nantai; they regularly had to be treated with offerings of food lest they get annoyed. The other soul, the spiritual (*shin*), leaves the body immediately after death to go on to its eternal destination – whether it is heaven, hell, nirvana or elsewhere.

I had already begun to understand this attitude while in Korea when I met a priest who was famous for diagnosing problems relating to various gravesites. His mission was to discover why the spirit of the person buried there was returning to bring bad luck, illness or family problems on his descendants. I wondered how, as a Christian, he could believe that a spirit who should have gone on to heaven or elsewhere after death would come back to bother the living. It was only when the multi-soul belief was explained to me that I could see it was just the earth or *gui* spirt that returned and had to be pacified.

Such thinking may seem exotic today; but it is not enough to simply dismiss it as weird. In Ireland do we not find shrines at places where accidents have happened – and flowers placed on graves? Did not the Irish also once believe that there were at least two souls – and that one stayed around possibly to haunt its old locality for some time? An eminent African scholar, John V. Taylor, found the same attitude to souls on that continent and refused to condemn it out of hand. Blaming our limited understanding on a lack of imagination, he wrote, 'By confining itself within the protective wall of the conscious and the rational, the modern mind has left untouched the great deep of the subliminal, and undreamed the glories of the elemental energies of humans.'

However, the main reason the local Chinese gave for forcing foreigners to live outside their cities was the belief that Westerners' lofty buildings such as churches ruined the local *feng shui*. This *feng shui* is the flow of wind and water that regulates the effects of positive influences (the impersonal force called *qi*) and, in practical terms, determines good or bad fortune for the area. It helps explain why the Irish Anglican mission in Fuzhou ended up on Nantai. Although foreigners, especially missionaries, regarded *feng shui* as superstitious, its influence continues even in modern China. Besides being based on the common-sense approach of building a house or digging a grave in an area that faces the sun, avoids underground water and is backed up by a wall or hill to deflect cold winds, *feng shui* has other merits – as practitioners of acupuncture can attest. What do they have in common? A belief in the life force – known as *qi*. This belief was also developed from practical observation, together with an intuition that Western scientists might find hard to accept – but an artist might admire.

On Hong Kong island, for instance, one prominent fifty-storey plush apartment block has a gap, high up in the centre, that is the equivalent of sixteen apartments. This 'hole' could be seen as an architectural embellishment – but in fact is in deference to the *feng-shui* professionals who detect and interpret the movement of *qi*. They diagnosed that the flow of *qi* (and good fortune) from the mountain behind would be blocked by the substantial building. So they suggested a 'hole' be created in the centre to let the *qi* flow through. The fact that Hong Kong's canny developers were willing to go along with the loss of the equivalent of sixteen commercial rents indicates the seriousness with which *qi* is still taken.

As this story might illustrate, Chinese 'science' has a different perspective than that of the science of the West, but one that is as widely believed and applied. While China has shown no difficulty in accepting the benefits of Western science, based on analytical reasoning and tangible experiments (as its recent impressive advances in transport, communications and industry are proof), enough of their heritage remains to remind them that there are other aspects of reality where such logic is irrelevant.

This was not the first nor the only incident in which this ancient Chinese belief tended to interfere with the establishment of Christian churches in Fuzhou. In the early 1840s, as China opened to the West, individual Irish Anglican missionaries went there in association with the London-based Church Missionary Society (CMS). Among the earliest was William Russell, who began his ministry in the east-coast treaty port of Ningbo in 1847 and was to become the first Anglican bishop in north China in 1872. To support his work, an organization distinct from the Church Missionary Society was founded by graduates of Trinity College Dublin in 1885. It became known as the Dublin University Far Eastern Mission (DUFEM). One of its better-known members, Richard Stewart, though a graduate of Trinity College Dublin, had become a member of the Church Missionary Society when he went to China. The son of a prominent Dublin family, he was studying law in London when he volunteered in 1875. He was ordained priest in St Paul's cathedral in 1878, married Louisa Smyly afterwards, and set out for China with her that September.

Appointed to a new theological college in Fuzhou, on arrival they immediately felt the tension between foreigners and the local people. The mission wanted to build a seminary on land they had leased from a Taoist temple on Wu-shih-shan hill in Fuzhou city. As the walls of the three-storey building rose, opposition increased among the locals on the grounds that it interfered with their *feng shui*. The Chinese officials offered an exchange with a property belonging to the former telegraph company on Nantai, but the missionaries refused. In August 1878 a mob attacked the site and burned the building. In the ensuing episode, known as the Wu-shih-shan Incident, the Consular Court decided that the temple had the right to take back the property; only then was the offer of the land on Nantai reluctantly accepted.

Stewart continued his work in and around Fuzhou, setting up schools in villages, sending the best students to Fuzhou High School for three years and encouraging interested graduates to join the Fuzhou Theological College. These activities came to an abrupt end in August 1895 when he took his family on holiday to the Huashan summer retreat, about seventy kilometres from the coast. There members of a local Buddhist vegetarian sect attacked the compound where the missionaries were staying, killing eleven people in what became known as the Kucheng Massacre. Among their victims were Richard Stewart, his wife, their two children and Helena Yellop the children's Irish nurse.

It is said that the story of their heroism inspired generations of Trinity students to volunteer for China.

Usually such a conflict of belief systems did not end so tragically. The Anglican missionaries in Fuzhou, like most newcomers to China, may have been slow to appreciate the Chinese attitude to law and leases or to *feng shui* and ghosts. But they quickly recognized the high regard in China for education.

After the Boxer Uprising in 1900 the imperial government accepted the need for educational and administrative reforms. The centuries-old civil service exam system, based on the teachings of Confucius, was finally abolished in 1906. In its place Western studies and foreign languages became increasingly popular. When the Reverend W. W. Pakenham-Walsh from Dublin came to Fuzhou with the CMS as chaplain to the British community in 1907, he founded St Mark's College on Nantai. Shortly afterwards it merged with a middle school and primary school to form Trinity College Fuzhou. St Mark's kept its identity as the Anglo-Chinese section of the school, using English as the medium for most of the classes. As the college's name implies, the majority of teachers were missionaries from Ireland serving with DUFEM. In 1928, when nationalism was sweeping the country, the last foreign school head resigned; but ironically the school continued to be extremely popular until the Communist Party came into power. After serving as No. 9 Middle School in the Mao era, Trinity School Fuzhou now operates as Fuzhou Foreign Language School – with relations with Trinity College Dublin and the DUFEM renewed.

Of course, Irish Anglican missionary activity extended well beyond Fuzhou and St Mark's College. Belfast-born John Hind became bishop of Fujian in 1897, implementing a policy of giving prominence to local clergy. Herbert Molony from Dublin became bishop of Zhejiang in 1907, a position he held for twenty years, taking a leading role in giving the Anglican Church in China its own independent constitution. By 1949, when the Dublin-born John Curtis (once an Irish soccer international), who had succeeded Molony twenty years earlier as bishop of Zhejiang, was expelled from China, he could leave confidently, saying, 'We are passing from mission relationships to Church relationships.'

Lasting Effects?

Today in Wuhan, Changchun and Fuzhou the footsteps of the Irish missionaries can still be traced in the legacy of hospitals, schools and churches they established. By 1954 all missionaries had been forced to leave China. But on their return home they shared happy memories of the people they knew and stories of a culture that at times appeared to be the opposite of their own Western upbringing: a topsy-turvy world in which books were read from back to front and people 'shake hands with themselves'.

Since the 1980s and the new opening up of China, these missionaries have renewed contact with the people and institutions they once knew, visiting and supporting them in their efforts to become updated and self-sufficient. In the meantime, they also had time to reflect on what they experienced in China, often discovering greater depths in its ancient culture.

Despite initial misgivings, it was in their daily interaction with ordinary people in different parts of China, through good times and bad, that the Irish excelled. They could instinctively recognize in the dignity and kindness and good intentions of the people a reassuring common humanity. If they examined those impressions more closely, in the image of the *junzi* 'complete person', the Irish may well have recalled the courtesy and sense of self-worth in elders they had known back home. In the openness of the Chinese people to wider, non-material realities and their disinclination to use black–white or true–false distinctions, they may have identified that creativity and large imagination that once gave the Irish a reputation as poets and storytellers. Finally, in the importance that Chinese people give to 'connections', the drawing on personal relationships and suspicion of strict laws and regulations, the Irish were on familiar ground. It was this ability to get on with people on an intuitive, rather than an institutional, level that enabled the Irish missionaries to make their greatest contribution in China.

Could such a search for instances in which traditional Chinese and Irish practices resemble each other now become an exercise in nostalgia? Both humanistic heritages are in danger of being overwhelmed by materialistic and individualistic trends. However, in comparing these civilizations, it is possible that China may have a better chance of pre-serving its distinctive people-centred characteristics than Ireland could on its own. China's strength in numbers, size and cultural longevity will help it retain the core of its traditional values. The country has a history of taking what it considers useful from the West and adapting it with 'Chinese characteristics' to become its own. Retaining those 'characteristics' has kept China united and unique.

After five years in China, Odoric and James of Ireland brought back glimpses 'from the other side of the earth' of a cultivated way of life that amazed Europe. The Irish missionaries of the twentieth century spent decades there and joined a growing number of Western scholars in return-ing with a more detailed description and a deeper appreciation of China's civilization and, in particular, its human and social values. If there is no one to continue this tradition, Ireland, and the rest of the Western world, will be the poorer for not having someone to challenge its assumption that it alone sets the standard for progress and human development.

Augustine Henry: A Botanical Pioneer in China, 1882–1900

Assumpta Broomfield

'No one in any age has contributed more to the
knowledge of Chinese plants than this scholarly
Irishman.' Ernest 'Chinese' Wilson

Who was this scholarly Irishman and how has he contributed to our knowledge of Chinese plants?

Augustine Henry is claimed as Irish on the basis that his father, Bernard Henry, had left Tyanee (now in Northern Ireland, a townland north of Portglenone, County Derry), aged 18 years, on a famine ship that sailed from Newry in 1848. After arriving in New York, Bernard joined the goldrush in California in 1849, then followed the goldrush to Australia, returning home to Ireland in 1854 without a huge fortune.

While visiting his sister Mary in Dundee, Scotland, he met and married Mary MacNamee, a Protestant who converted to Catholicism. There they ran a small grocery shop. In 1856 their first daughter was born, followed the next year, on 2 July 1857, by Augustine. A month later the family moved back to Ireland, settling in Cookstown, County Tyrone, where Bernard began a very successful flax-trading business. The family increased: by 1871 another four boys and three girls had been born. Sadly, Mary died soon after the birth of her son Daniel, leaving behind nine children under 15 years of age. The children spent much of their time with their grandmother, Anne, in their ancestral town of Tyanee.

Augustine attended Cookstown Academy, where he excelled. There he met a fellow pupil who had been self-taught and attended the academy for two years. Now aspiring to attend Queen's College Galway, the friend had won a scholarship and 'entered triumphantly, red muffler and all, the first working man to take a place in the College'. Inspired, Augustine began to teach himself Latin and by this means also managed to gain entry to Queen's College Galway. Studying natural science and philosophy, Henry graduated in 1877 with a first-class honours degree and a gold medal in the BA examination. The following year he received an MA in medicine from Queen's College Belfast and then spent one year at a London hospital.

Back in Belfast, Henry's old professor told him that Sir Robert Hart wanted a young man with some knowledge of medicine to be stationed in China as a customs officer, with a salary of £420 per annum. With this appointment in mind, Henry went to Edinburgh to sit special medical exams (at double fee) and was duly acclaimed as qualified in medicine on 10 August 1881. Then, having also sat and passed the required exam, Henry was formally accepted into the customs service.

Henry would have already heard of the famous Robert Hart, if only as a fellow Irishman who had blazed the way for what was to become a lifelong career in China. Born in 1835 in Portadown, County Armagh, Hart, like Henry, identified as Irish and, as the eldest of twelve children, was the first son of a large family. After one year at a Wesleyan school in England and another at Wesleyan Connexion School in Dublin, in 1850, aged 15 years, Hart entered Queen's College Belfast, graduating three years later with a BA. In later life, Hart always tried to recruit fellow Irishmen, particularly those, like Henry, from the Queen's Colleges throughout Ireland – and if possible, like Henry, possessing a medical degree.

Robert Hart's own route to employment by the Chinese government was not an obvious one. The year following his graduation, Queen's College nominated him for a post in the British Consular Service as an interpreter in China. During the time he was stationed in Hong Kong, Ningpo (Ningbo) and then Canton (Guangzhou). There Hart took lessons in the Chinese language. During this time, the Qing Dynasty government decided to reorganize their native customs service, which they found both inefficient and corrupt, by hiring foreigners. Thus five years after his arrival, Hart was recruited from the British Consular Service to take up a post as Deputy Commissioner at Canton in the Chinese Imperial Maritime Customs Service (CIMCS). Such was the regard in which he was held by his Chinese employers that in 1863, aged only 28 years, Hart was promoted to Inspector General.

His career was built on his reputation for incorruptibility – and well as his talent for innovation. Hart's main responsibilities included: collecting customs for the Chinese government; expanding the customs stations to include more sea and river ports and some inland stations; standardizing its operations; and ensuring high standards of honesty and efficiency among the staff. He also proposed a modern postal service and recommended that the collecting of internal taxes be added to the CIMCS duties. For a young man such as Henry, interested in a variety of jobs as well as experience of different areas of China, this was an ideal career. Hart also provided his men with an impeccable role model. Friendly with both Chinese and Western officials, Hart was unusual as an official insofar as he encouraged mutual understanding by establishing in 1862 the Tongwen Guan (School of Combined Learning) in Peking (Beijing) to enable Chinese people to learn languages, cultures and science for future diplomatic needs. Known as the most trusted foreigner in China, Hart retained his title of Inspector General until 1911, although he had already left China in 1908.

This was the service that Augustine Henry had successfully joined. The Irish connection continued when Henry and Mr Lowry, another recruit, newly arrived in Hong Kong in 1881, called on the chief judge of Hong Kong, Judge Russell, also a graduate of Queen's College Belfast. Russell in turn introduced them to the chief manager of the Hong Kong Shanghai Bank, Mr Thomas Jackson, also Irish. Jackson remarked, 'I suppose you are not very flush of money?' and told the cashier to 'give these two gentlemen whatever money they want'. They borrowed £50 each. An important lesson in the efficacy of the Irish network abroad, this incident was not forgotten by Henry, who afterwards did all his business through this bank, dictating the story many years later to his second wife Alice. Henry and Lowry then travelled on to Shanghai, where the Consul General was yet another Irishman, Patrick Hughes from Newry, County Down.

Taking up his position in July 1881, Henry found the weather extremely hot. Office hours were ten till four with an hour off for lunch. Henry, however, rose between five and six o'clock and (in the words of his journal) 'rode off on a pony outside the settlement, returned to bath and breakfast'. The winter was spent in Shanghai, where Henry became a member of the Shanghai Club, went riding, attended pony racing (imported from Mongolia) and played tennis.

On 10 March 1882 he left for his next posting to Ichang (Yichang), arriving there on 16 April 1882. Ichang was (and still is) a busy port well upriver on the Yangtze (Chang Jiang) in Hubei Province near the famous Three Gorges. In 1877 it had become a treaty port as well as an important trading post. At this point, all trade back and forth from China passed through the customs service officials. Outgoing products included plants used in traditional Chinese medicine such as *Rheum officinale* (Chinese rhubarb) and elk horn, raw yellow silk, white wax, hides, musk and opium. Incoming products included Manchester goods such as cotton and velveteen. Fishing was very important; on the far bank, as Henry reported, the Chinese had tamed otters to catch fish. The town of Ichang had a population of thirty thousand, with the 'foreign compound' sited right on the banks of the river. Within the compound were both the British and German consulates. Also based there was a Church of Scotland under the Reverend G. Cockburn, whose wife was the first European woman to live in Ichang. A Roman Catholic Franciscan mission and a small convent were also based there.

Henry was kept busy with his customs and medical duties and after work he played tennis, cards and went for walks. The following entries for this period can be found in his diary:

25 May 1882 – went for walk looking for fossils with a colleague and took Chinese lesson from local teacher, Mr. Teng. Wrote letters to Miss Evelyn Gleeson of Benown House, Athlone, Ireland.
14 October 1882 – went on trip with acting British Consul E. L. Allen to the Dome via Monastery valley. Went boating up river to the Glen of Three Pilgrims, six miles away and to the Glen of Goat.

11 Nov 1883 – trip to Nanto [Liantuo] and the next day from Nanto
to Chinkang Shan Taoist Temple.
22 Aug 1884 – order Bentley's Botany
25 Nov 1884 crossed river – botanised about Shil-Liu_Lung.

Henry got into the study of botany through his medical studies,
becoming interested in the native use of plants for therapeutic purposes.
By the following March, Henry was writing to Sir Joseph Dalton
Hooker, then director of the Royal Botanic Gardens, Kew, including
seeds of the varnish tree, *Rhus verniciflua*, the source of Chinese lacquer,
with the following message:

> A good number of medicines are grown about here and there seems
> to be a fair number of interesting plants and, as this part of China is
> not known to botanists (at any rate, as compared with the south and
> also the northern and maritime provinces), interesting specimens
> might be obtained. I know very little botany and have scarcely any
> books of reference. However, I should be glad to collect specimens
> and forward them to you if you think they would be useful.[1]

The response from Kew was nothing less than enthusiastic. At the
time, virtually nothing was known of the flora of central China;
the bulk of the dried specimens in the herbarium at Kew came
from the eastern coastal regions.[2] With such a reception, Henry's
pastime soon became a passionate pursuit. Henry set about his new
hobby with his usual scrupulous methodology, making contact with
leading Chinese plant hunters of the day. In April and June 1885, for
instance, Henry received letters from Henry Fletcher Hance, British
vice consul at Whampoa (Huangpu) in Guangdong Province in
south-eastern China.

With an herbarium including 22,437 specimens, Hance was an
acknowledged expert on Chinese plants. In his letter he recommended
Franchet's two volume *Plantae Davidianae ex Sinarum imperio,* the first
volume of which had been published in Paris the previous year. He also
advised on how to dry specimens and protect them from insect damage.
Henry recognized how important this advice was in dictating how

leaves, flowers and seeds of plants were to be collected, dried between sheets of paper and pressed. These specimens could then be used by taxonomists to describe and name each new species or subspecies – preserved for all future reference in an herbarium.

In November 1885 Henry sent his first consignment of 1,073 dried plant specimens and 183 fruits and seeds to Kew. After it arrived (in the spring of 1886), each specimen was scrupulously numbered and dated, along with a record of their Chinese names, locations, habits, habitats and economic uses. A note in the Kew archives by Professor Daniel Oliver reads, 'This collection is one of the most important which we have ever received from the interior of China.' It contained 120 new species, subspecies, varieties and forms. Among this collection were plants that were to become essentials of every good garden in Ireland, such as *Parthenocissus henryana*, the beautiful marbled climber and *Viburnum rhytidophyllum* with its deeply veined leaves. For Henry had quickly realized that the climate and terrain of central China was such that its native plants were hardy enough to suit the British Isles. By now he had also become interested in ornamental as well as medicinal and economic plants.

As a result of these early collecting activities, Augustine Henry's material dominated the first of three volumes of *Index Florae Sinensis* (1886–1905), published by the Linnean Society of London.[3] The authors were Francis Blackwell Forbes and William Botting Hemsley, assistant keeper of Kew's herbarium and fellow of the Linnean Society. It was to take almost twenty years to complete. For Henry, the timing of this first volume could not have been better, as, over the ensuing years, his specimens were both lodged and registered in probably the best resourced botanic institute and garden in the English-speaking world.

However, during this early period in Ichang, from 1885–7, Augustine Henry's own collecting was initially 'limited to a radius of ten–fifteen miles and to altitudes not exceeding 3,000 ft. The summer heat often reached 100 degrees in the shade, but although it was bitterly cold in winter, with snow, there was rarely any trace of frost.'[4] During this time, he wrote an article, published in 1888, entitled 'Chinese Names of Plants' in the *Journal of the China Branch of the Royal Asiatic Society*. While the scientific names were mainly the names received from Kew, the colloquial Chinese names were as used in two Chinese works, *Chih wu ming* and *Pen Ts'ao kong mu*. Over six hundred plants were named; here are just two interesting examples:

> 10. Ch'a, 茶, *Camellia Thea* [tea] … the best native tea is produced in the *Lo T'ien ch'i* neighbourhood. Tea for the foreign market is produced in the districts of the south.
>
> 115. Ho shou wu, 何首烏, *Polygonum multiflorum* [Tuber Fleeceflower] Thbg. When the root assumes a likeness to the human figure, it sells for a very large sum and is deemed an invaluable drug.

In fact, all the examples are interesting, and the publication of these names cleared up a lot of confusion between their Chinese and English names.

In April 1888, the year his grandmother died, Henry was granted six months' leave from his customs duties. He left Ichang to embark on a three-month tour of the mountains to the north and south of the Yangtze River. When Henry and his collectors set out on this first trip, they were accompanied as far as Changyang County by Mr Antwerp E. Pratt. While Pratt was mainly interested in zoological specimens, he was persuaded by Henry to engage a local man whom he had trained to collect botanical specimens, a collection also later sent to Kew. Pratt, in a preface to his book, *To the Snows of Tibet through China* (1892), thanks Henry (among many others) for the courtesy and help he had given.

Henry, now accompanied by a number of local men, set off for Changyang, Patung (Badong) and the southern part of Wushan district in Sichuan Province, a trip that was both exciting and rewarding. Changyang was mountainous, with deep valleys and gorges – and dangerous with wild pigs, tigers and leopards. Henry was too busy to write up his diary, but the consequent collection of specimens was astonishing. Pratt did write about the fragrance of the honeysuckle – and the rhododendrons growing luxuriantly with large, white, fragrant blossoms. Three trees found there – the *Sorbus helmsleyi*, a whitebeam; *Acer henryi*, the Henry maple; and *Poliothysis sinensis*, Chinese pearlbloom – are now grown at the National Botanic Gardens, Glasnevin in Dublin. *Liriodenron chinense*, the Chinese tulip tree, was discovered on this trip; previously it was thought to be the same as the American species. *Paulownia fargesii* and *P. tomentosa*, both known as foxglove trees, were also collected. The latter grows very well in Glasnevin, as does yet another remarkable tree discovered on the expedition, *Sycopsis sinensis*, the evergreen Chinese fighazel.

The list of previously unknown species of trees from that trip is long and absorbing. But perhaps the most significant discovery was that of *Davidia involucrata* var. *wilmoriniana*: a tree adorned with large white bracts (a modified leaf), hence its nickname, the Handkerchief Tree. Describing the moment when he first saw what the Chinese call the Dove Tree, Henry recalls that it was while

> riding his pony through a river valley when he spotted a single, spectacular tree flowering near the base of a large cliff. As he was later to relate, the scene was one of the strangest sights he ever witnessed in China. It seemed as though the branches had been draped in thousands of ghostly, white handkerchiefs'.[5]

It was 17 May 1888. As he later reports, by sending two trusted native plant collectors to the spot just south of the famous Yangtze gorges in late autumn, he was also able to secure its fruits, the first ever seen by a European. Henry was only the second Westerner ever to spot this tree and the first to discover this specific variety. In 1889, a specimen from Henry was received with some excitement at Kew Gardens. At the time, Henry could not know that this single tree was to initiate the greatest era of plant introductions from western and central China.

Henry returned to Yichang for a few days and then set out again. Travelling through Tung hu, Paokang, Fang and Wushan, he went north of the Yangtze. In a letter to Sir William Thistleton-Dyer, written on 9 October 1888, Henry reported that

> I have a just returned from my second trip, having been away almost two-and-half months. I travelled due north from Ichang till I reached the range separating the basins of the Yangtze and Han rivers and then I made my way along the range westwards as far as Szechuan [Sichuan], striking then the Yangtze and the Hupeh-Szechuan [Hubei-Sichuan] boundary line. I returned two or three days ago down the rapids.

In a later memoir, Henry described this descent:

> I hardly enjoyed this trip, which only took ten hours of actual sailing time, as the river was in high flood. I was in a small boat, with twenty of my men and a precious freight of a dozen or more boxes of dried plants, and I knew the slightest accident, a wrong turn of the sweep, might involve the loss of these boxes.[6]

In his letter, Henry also wrote that many interesting conifers occurred in this zone, as well as four *Ribes* (shrubs with berries, one being an excellent gooseberry), a *Betula* (a species of hardwood trees that includes birches, alders, hazels and hornbeam), many *Acers* (maples), a curious *Rubi* (unidentified), a *Fragaria* (strawberry) and many roses and viburnums. He also pointed out that in these elevated regions many important Chinese drugs could be found, of which the origin had been hitherto unknown. Rhubarb – used in China for medical purposes – and *Tang shen* (Deng Shen or the dried root of 'poor man's ginseng'), another important drug, were common. Along with these were many other significant herbal medicines, details of which he would send on with the specimens. 'I had a very pleasant trip, being on excellent terms with the people,' Henry wrote, remarking that, 'No foreigner, not even the Roman Catholic missionaries, had ever been in these parts before.'[7]

As a result of these expeditions, Henry had created an enormous collection, extremely rich in new specimens (ten new species of *Acer* alone). Many others had also sent collections to Kew to be identified by the noted botanist William Hemsley and included in this new index of Chinese plants, among them Reverend Ernst Faber who had collected on Mount Omei. Also arriving at Kew during this period were other collections from Mr Antwerp Pratt and his Chinese gatherer in 1889 and 1890. Collected from the area of western China on the border of Eastern Tibet, near the town of Tachienlu, Kanding, these contained at least five hundred new species, later to be supplemented by 150 more from this same area identified by Prince Henry d'Orleans. But among all these new species, there was not a single new genus – whereas Henry and the Reverend Faber (whom Henry had first met in Ichang in 1887) between them had already documented about twenty-five new genera.

As William Hemsley observed, when he started the actual listing of all known plants from China in 1882, almost nothing of the botany of the central and western provinces of China had been so far documented. Although Mr Franchet of the Paris Museum National d'Histoire Naturelle had published *Plantae Davidianae,* it had contained only 'a comparatively small number of novelties and among them no new genera'.[8] Henry was able to collect so extensively because he trained local men to collect and press specimens for him – we know this because he kept accounts of their payment – starting with one man in 1885, two men in 1886 and ultimately four in 1888. That autumn, he dispatched them to amass a collection of new fruits and seeds to be sent on to Kew. At Kew, while Professor Daniel Oliver had drawings made of the seed of the *Davidia,* he failed to have them sown – even though two years later he would write that '*Davidia* is a tree almost deserving a special mission to Western China with a view to its introduction to European gardens'. In 1888 that mission was fulfilled when the Handkerchief Tree did in fact become the sole quest of the first expedition by perhaps China's most famous Western plant hunter, Ernest 'Chinese' Wilson.

By the next spring, in April 1889, Henry left mainland China, having been transferred to Hainan, a tropical island in the South China Sea. His departure from Ichang was marked by both sadness and celebration. *The North China Herald and Supreme Court and Consular Gazette* reported on 15 March 1889 that

> Dr. Henry left Ichang today after nearly seven years' stay, having had nearly all the primroses of Son Yew-tung brought down in his honour and walking down into the river bed between a double row of crackers and Roman candles all one after another lighting up and exploding, as he passed along the sands. These fireworks were the tribute from the Chinese part of the customs staff. The little European community all dined each other in his honour to the very last. He will be greatly missed, having shown kindness onto every man.

Henry travelled to Hoihow (Haikou), capital of Hainan, via Hong Kong. The mountains of Hainan were then covered in dense tropical forests; tropical storms were frequent throughout the summer months. Henry's main collecting was done around Hoihow, where many fruits and vegetables were abundant (for example, guava, papayas, mung beans and sweet Chinese yams). There the *Nelumbo nucifera* or sacred lotus also flourished. Again, Henry recruited native collectors, amassing over 740 specimens. Then suffering from malaria and in poor health, Henry left for Hong Kong after only four months.

Having been granted two years' leave to regain his health, Henry left Hong Kong on a circuitous route to Ireland, travelling via Japan, where he met the Japanese botanist Jinzo Matsumura, and continuing on by way of San Francisco, Chicago and Toronto to arrive eventually in Cobh, County Cork on 17 October 1889. Then returning north and home to Tyanee, County Derry, he corresponded with other plant collectors including William Richard Carles of the British Consular Service in China and Père Delavay, who was stationed in north-west Yunnan. Père Delavay had gone to China with the Société des Missions Etrangères de Paris in 1867 and served in Guangdong Province in the south-east. Back in France, in 1881, Delavay met Adrien René Franchet, who persuaded him to collect for the Muséum National d'Histoire Naturelle. While serving in north-west Yunnan in the years 1882–95, he sent 200,000 herbarium specimens to the Paris museum, of which Franchet estimated that there were more than 4,000 species, 1,500 being entirely new to science.

In 1889, still restless, within a month Henry was off to visit Kew. There he was surprised to be welcomed as a celebrity by the director, Sir William Thistleton-Dyer; by John Gilbert Baker, who had described his ferns; by Professor Daniel Oliver, Keeper of the Herbarium; by Doctor Otto Stapf; and by William Botting Hemsley, who had worked on most of Henry's specimens and was the author of *Index Florae Sinensis*. During a special dinner in his honour that evening, Henry met many of the most important people in botany and horticulture, including Sir Harry Veitch, who had followed Henry's success in China. The Veitch family had for generations sent plant collectors throughout the world – to the Americas, Australia, India, Japan and China. Later, influenced by Henry, it was the Veitch family who sent the most successful plant collector of them all, Ernest 'Chinese' Wilson, to China.

Now in London, Henry spent eighteen months sorting out his own and other collections of plants at Kew: a necessary task, as there was a backlog – and he was able to read the Chinese notes, a very useful skill. This experience, under the direction of Hemsley, served Henry well some years later when he wrote (with Henry John Elwes) *The Trees of Great Britain and Ireland*.

Throughout his time in China, Henry had stayed in contact with Evelyn Gleeson from Athlone. In 1891, while visiting her, he met her friend Caroline Orridge from London, and on 20 June 1891, they married. They travelled to China, where they were based in Shanghai. But by then Caroline had become extremely ill with tuberculosis. Henry requested a transfer to Taiwan, where he thought the weather would suit her. But as there was still no improvement in her health, she eventually left in 1894 with Henry's sister for Colorado, where Henry hoped she would recover.

During this period, Henry also published *Notes on Economic Botany of China* in 1893. Printed by the Presbyterian Mission Press, its opening words were an appeal to other amateur botanists, as 'Missionaries and others living in the interior are often in a position to make enquiries concerning the natural production of China, the results of which would be of great service to science.' In its seventy pages, Henry explains why it is so important to have samples of plants so that they can be identified correctly – giving many examples, such as,

> Fruits of two species, very similar in appearance, may be quite distinct in properties. Thus the 'false star-aniseed' of Japan, produced by *Illicium religiosum*, S&Z., is not only non-fragrant but is also extremely poisonous, whereas the 'true star-aniseed' of Kwangtung and Annam, produced by *Illicium vernum*, H.K. fil et T., is fragrant, wholesome and useful.

It is not clear how or if any of the missionaries targeted in this appeal responded; but it does throw light on their often-neglected role in transmitting important information about China to the West.

While stationed on the island of Taiwan (1892–4), Henry was given a new position as an assistant in the Customs Service, having given up his medical duties. With Caroline being so ill, he was sad and depressed – in the years afterwards, he worried whether he could have done more for her. But, as always, the plant collecting continued. In May 1893, Henry contacted one Hosea Ballou Morse, a Harvard graduate and commissioner in the Customs Service, stationed at Tamsui, Taiwan, until the Japanese invasion in 1895. Morse was a Canadian-born American who later became a British citizen. He is best known for his renowned books *The International Relations of the Chinese Empire*, a three-volume chronicle of the relations of the Qing Dynasty with Western countries, and *The Chronicles of the East India Company Trading to China, 1635 to 1834*. Under appeal, Morse agreed to collect specimens for Henry. While Henry already had a number of local people working for him under the supervision of Mr Schuser, a lighthouse keeper, he acknowledged Morse's help in his published *List of Taiwanese Plants*.

In March 1886, the Botanic Gardens in Kew published *A Report on the Botany of Formosa*, mentioning that, for this exercise, 'Mr. Augustine Henry's notes possessed special value'. In these notes, Henry indicates that he had sent over two thousand numbers (dried samples) with duplicates to Kew, comprising a thousand species. He describes several of these plants, including *Mangifera indica*, the mango; *Nephelium longana*, the longan; and *Ficus retusa*, the common banyan tree. He also mentions all the earlier plant collectors: Wilford, Oldham, Swinhoe, Ford, Campbell, Playfair and (notably) two Irishmen – Hancock and Watters – while pointing out that Playfair's collection had been omitted from the *Index Florae Sinensis*.

By May 1894, Henry had also written to Professor Charles Sprague Sargent, the founding director of the Arnold Arboretum of Harvard University in Boston, offering his personal herbarium for sale. Although he now hoped to resign from the Customs Service and join his wife in Colorado, the Customs Service granted Henry only one year's leave – and not to be taken until November. In the meantime, Taiwan was under threat of invasion by Japan. In September, just as Henry was about to depart to join Caroline in Colorado, the dreadful news came of her death on the twenty-fifth of that month. So when he finally did head for Colorado, it was to be consoled by his sister, not to be finally reunited with his wife. Later Henry named the small primrose he discovered in Yunnan *Carolinella henryi* to commemorate her.

During his stay in America, Henry paid a visit to Professor Sargent of the Arnold Arboretum. Established in 1872, its mission was to grow indigenous and exotic plants as well as to increase knowledge of woody plants through research and education. There Henry sold a number of his specimens to Sargent, who redistributed them to the principal botanic gardens in America.

When he did finally return to London, Henry worked once again with Hemsley identifying Chinese plants. While there Henry also took up the study of law, becoming a member of the Middle Temple. As his second wife, Alice, later said, 'He wore the gown and ate the dinners' (requirements for all who qualify as barristers in Great Britain).

In the autumn of 1895, Henry returned to his duties in Shanghai, only to be posted in 1896 to Yunnan in south-west China: its sixth largest province and its richest area botanically, with over half of China's flowering plants growing there. It is also home to one-third of China's ethnic groups. He travelled there from Hanoi through Laocai on the Chinese–Vietnamese border and from there on to the old walled city of Mengtze (Mengzi). Today the customs house where Henry was to work is a museum, displaying artefacts, documents and photographs of the history of the building. The town, with a population of around ten thousand, was surrounded by the Daweishan mountain range, covered in dense forests. Henry soon began botanizing, with the help of a native plant collector, 'Old Ho'. In a letter to Kew, dated 5 September 1896, Henry wrote:

> I have just had a native collecting in the mountains south of the Red River, near the French frontier, and he has brought back from the virgin forests of a high mountain about 100 interesting species … He has also brought me undoubted *wild* tea. Hitherto, the tea plant had been found wild only in Assam, the cases of its spontaneity recorded from China being very doubtful. The present specimens are above suspicion, coming from virgin forest, and at an immense distance from any tea cultivation, the nearest being P'u-erh, 200 miles west. Bretschneider (in *Botanicon Sinicum* part II., p. 130) has some remarks

on the antiquity of tea in China, and it is not till the sixth or seventh century that it came into general use (*BMI*, 1897).

While the countryside immediately around Mengtze was not so rich in botanical specimens, after two days' travel in all other directions their variety was phenomenal. Old Ho had already brought back *Lysimachia*, whose leaves were used for scenting hair oil, some new varieties of *Lauraceae* (laurels) and several ferns. The forests had bears – a sign of virgin forest. Henry was not to be daunted. Mules were plentiful, making travel relatively easy; to his delight, almost every day Henry came across plants he had never seen before.

In these mountains Henry also came across three ethnic groups: Shans, Lolos (Yi) and Miao-tzu. He was particularly interested in the Lolos:'I like their looks and way of talking'. Their system of writing, still in use, had come from a highly civilized culture, and they had preserved manuscripts that had a writing system quite different from regular Chinese. Henry visited them often in their jungle village of Simao, not only to botanize but also to compile a Yi language dictionary. After one such expedition he wrote in a letter to Kew, dated 23 February 1897, 'I have just returned from an exceedingly interesting trip to the country south of the Red River, a district ruled over by a hereditary chief, who treated me with great kindness' (*BMI*, 1897). Some years later, in 1903, Henry wrote a paper entitled 'The Lolos and Other Tribes of Western China'. Published in the *Journal of the Anthropological Institute of Great Britain and Ireland*, it proves Henry was as interested in rare people as in rare plants.

In that same letter to Kew, Henry described plants he collected on the Ailaoshan range of mountains, reporting that

> I secured a magnificent Rhododendron, a Magnolia (both great trees), three Camellias, Stuartia [a small group of flowering trees and shrubs closely related to camellias], etc. There was a Daphne (indica?), a shrub with deliciously scented white flowers, a Primula [primrose] at the summit and many, many more. Along the Red River, the vegetation was tropical, with bananas, tomatoes, papayas as well as the strangest tree, *Dolichandrone caudefelina*, which had pods

almost a metre long, with a dense covering of thick brown hair – like the tail of an animal.

While Henry anticipated that there would be three thousand species in the year's collection, he had already numbered and labelled 660 distinct species. All in all, Henry estimated that his collection would reach five thousand species, and that, together with Delavay's five thousand species, about ten thousand species of the flora of Yunnan would be identified by the twentieth century. Among the bulbous plants he found was *Lilium giganteum*, now known to us as *Cardiocrinum giganteum*, one of the most treasured lilies now grown in the West. Henry observed in some awe that while 'Orchids are very numerous, I could go on indefinitely' about other species. He also described seeing deer, weasels (small black ones as well as large flying ones), partridges, pheasants, snakes, a tiger and a leopard. But he despaired that he did not have enough time, as what was needed above all was time and patience. Consequently, writing in a letter to Kew on 19 July 1897, he advised that what 'I would suggest, so great is the variety and beauty of the Chinese flora, and so fit are the plants for the European climate, that an effort ought to be made to send out a small expedition' (*BMI*, 1897).

Meanwhile, Henry had received a collection of four hundred species from Hosea Ballou Morse, the customs official now stationed at Lungchow in Kwangsi (Guangxi) Province. At the same time, Mr Bons d'Anty, stationed south of Szemao (Simao), was also collecting plants for him. By the time Henry himself was transferred to Szemao in 1898, he had dispatched thirty-two cases of herbarium specimens, which were being sent both to Kew in London and the Arnold Arboretum in the States.

On the eighteen-day journey to Szemao, Henry travelled through the forests near the Pa Tien River, home of the wild peacock and the jungle fowl, the ancestor of domestic fowl. By then Acting Chief Commissioner of Customs, the Emperor's representative in Szemao – with the status of a mandarin – upon entering the town Henry was escorted in a sedan chair, with crackers exploding and flags waving, surrounded by three detachments of soldiers. In corresponding with

Professor Sargent, Henry described a distinct regional flora, surprised at how different it was to that of Mengtze (Mengzi). But he found even more interesting the extraordinary diversity of the human inhabitants: 'there are four or five distinct races', he observed. But as Henry had acquired extra responsibilities in his new posting, most of the plant collecting was now done by Old Ho.

Two years later, in April 1899, Old Ho died of malaria. As Henry wrote to his friend Evelyn Gleeson shortly afterwards:

> He was most honest and hard-working and his end was so sad. He died on the roadside while trying to get back. His comrades left the body, tried to get the village to take it in, but the villagers refused, so they came on here. I sent out a party who brought the body in and he is now grandly coffined (which is the only serious question in China) and tomorrow being a lucky day he will be buried. It is impossible to replace this honest man.[9]

Indeed, nearly all the best finds from Yunnan Province could be attributed to him. In later years, Henry made sure that Old Ho was commemorated in *Senecio hoi* (a species of daisy) and *Schefflera hoi* (the dwarf umbrella tree), according to the customary way of honouring those who discover new plants.

In February of that year, during an official two-week tour around Szemao, shocked at the extent of deforestation, Henry again urged both Kew and the Arnold Arboretum to send out a trained collector. Professor Sargent wanted Henry himself to take up the position, but Henry declined, saying a young man was needed. Through persistence and pressure from Henry, Kew convinced the London nursery company of James H. Veitch and Sons Ltd. to send out a Kew-trained collector. That man was Ernest Henry 'Chinese' Wilson (1876–1930), a 24-year-old student gardener at Kew, who had trained at Birmingham Botanic Garden. The instructions from Veitch to Wilson were as follows:

> The object of the journey is to collect a quantity of seeds of a plant the name of which is known to us. This is the object − do not dissipate time, energy or money on anything else. In furtherance of

this you will first endeavour to visit Dr Augustine Henry and obtain precise data as to the habitat of this particular plant and information on the flora of central China in general.

The plant was *Davidia involucrata* var. *vilmoriniana*, or the Handkerchief Tree, rediscovered by Henry in 1888.

Wilson's journey was interrupted by floods, which necessitated changes in travel plans – and by civil disturbances aimed at foreigners, which were to culminate in the Boxer Rebellion of 1900. At Mengtze, the house of the Commissioner of Customs had been destroyed by fire, its occupants forced to flee in their nightclothes. Arriving the morning afterwards, Wilson later described the aftermath of the drama. 'I saw suspended from the branches of a tree, wooden cages containing the heads of five of the rioters. Later I met a posse of soldiers bringing in another gruesome looking head.' When Wilson did eventually meet Henry (fortunately not in Mengtze but in quieter Simao) on 24 September 1899, Henry drew a map on a half-page of a notebook showing the location of the *Davidia* tree. Impressed with the energy, enthusiasm, knowledge and good humour of Wilson, he and Henry became lifelong friends.

Finally, for his last posting, Henry was promoted and transferred back to Mengtze in Yunnan, where he remained until he retired on 31 December 1900, 'the last day of the 19th century'. Returning to Europe, Henry stayed for a year in London, where he worked on his Chinese collections. While there he befriended William Jackson Bean, Assistant Curator at Kew. He also visited Arthur K. Bulley in Liverpool. Bulley, who had written animated letters to Henry in China requesting various seeds, was later to sponsor George Forrest and Frank Kingdon-Ward on Chinese expeditions. Through his many contacts, Henry was also remarkably successful in persuading other colleagues to send more collectors to China. David Fairchild, Head of Plant Introduction at the Department of Agriculture, USA, for instance, wrote, 'The information which he gave me determined me to send explorers into China.' Both Frank N. Meyer and the famous Joseph Rock were among those sent out as the result of Henry's representations.

In October 1902 Henry moved to France to enrol in a course at a forestry school in Nancy. The following April, he was visited there by Henry John Elwes, who implored him to research and co-author *The Trees of Great Britain and Ireland*. Elwes was an English landowner and distinguished naturalist who was eager to finance and organize publication of an authoritative reference work on trees. Accepting his invitation, good specimens of all trees, native and non-native, throughout Britain and Ireland were identified, visited and measured. Individual histories were noted, growing conditions and habitat written up, the trees photographed. Based on their extensive travels – throughout every country in Europe, nearly all the states of America, through Canada, Chile, China, India, Japan and western Siberia – the authors could assert that Britain and Ireland contained a greater number of fine trees from the temperate regions of the world than any other country. In relation to historic trees in Ireland – which had to this point been entirely neglected – its seven volumes (appearing one by one between 1906 and 1913) remain, to this day, 'the most remarkable books on trees that have ever been published'.[10]

In 1907, Henry was appointed Reader and later Professor of Forestry in the School of Forestry at Cambridge University. His marriage in 1908 to Alice Brunton began a lengthy period of domestic happiness, during which Henry decided to return to Ireland where, in 1913, he was appointed Professor of Forestry at the newly established Chair of Forestry at the Royal College of Science, Dublin (now part of University College Dublin), a position he held until he retired in 1926. Proud of his Irish ancestry, Henry could trace his own family back to the O'Innerigh clan in the twelfth century. It was not surprising, then, that during his time in Dublin he befriended many of those associated with the Celtic Revival movement. Among these were George Russell (known as 'AE'), the artist and poet, as well as the painter Jack B. Yeats (whose brother was William Butler Yeats). He lent support to his friend Evelyn Gleeson when she established the Dun Emer Centre, which furthered Irish crafts and printmaking; and he is said to have admired the work of Horace Plunkett and the co-operative movement he founded.

During this period, too, Henry was to be bestowed with many honours: MA Honoris Causa, Cambridge University; Victoria Medal of Honour, Royal Horticultural Society; Veitch Memorial Medal, Royal Horticultural Society; Fellow of the Linnean Society; Corresponding

Member of the Académie d'Agriculture de France; and Member of the Royal Irish Academy.

But perhaps, for him, the best tribute of all came in 1929 from China:

> To
> Augustine Henry
> Through whose assiduous Botanical Exploration
> of Central and South-Western China,
> the Knowledge of our Flora
> has been greatly extended.
> The Second Fascicle of the *Icones Plantarum Sinicarum* is
> Respectfully Dedicated,
> Professor H. H. Hu and N.Y. Chun 1929
> Beijing, China

When Professor H. H. Hu, Fan Memorial Institute of Biology, Beijing, China wrote to Henry about this dedication, the letter became a personal tribute to Henry's work, remarking that

> As a pioneer and veteran botanist of western China, you have not only added to the world much scientific knowledge of the Chinese flora; but you have set up a great example for Chinese botanical students. This dedication is our humble appreciation of what you have so nobly achieved.

Augustine Henry died after a short illness on 23 March 1930 at his home in Ranelagh, Dublin, Ireland.

During his lifetime, he had brought to the attention of the West the beauty and variety of the Chinese flora. With his genial personality and ability to work with others of every nationality, station and background, Henry had also brought together the work of many disparate, enthusiastic naturalists.

Today Augustine Henry will be remembered as a towering figure in Irish forestry, a champion of plant hunters and a celebrated plant hunter himself. Ireland's credentials in global botany are, at least in part, endorsed by his pioneering work. One may view some of his collections in the National Botanic Gardens, Glasnevin, Dublin, home

John Scotus Eriugena as imagined for the old Irish £5 bank note. In the background is a biblical text from the Book of Durrow, copied by monks c. 650–700 CE. Specimen. This image is reproduced courtesy of the Central Bank of Ireland.

Departure of Friar Odoric and James of Ireland to the East in April 1318.

Bishop Edward Galvin baptizing a child with grandparents looking on. Courtesy of The Missionary Society of St Columban.

Fr Thomas Quinlan from Tipperary with the Columban College hurling team in Hanyang, China, c. 1920s. Courtesy of The Missionary Society of St Columban.

The Yangtze River, bursting its banks in the spring of 1931, flooded an area twice the size of Ireland. Bishop Edward Galvin was put in charge of the official emergency rescue operations. Courtesy of The Missionary Society of St Columban.

Irish Columban sisters visiting a rural parish in China in the 1930s.
Courtesy of The Missionary Sisters of St Columban.

Dr Sally Wolfe with a Chinese baby girl whose feet had been bound.
Courtesy of Jane Wright.

Augustine Henry, aged 41, in the courtyard of the customs quarters at Simao, leaning on his Irish blackthorn walking stick. Courtesy of Dr Barbara Philips.

One of Henry's plant collectors, said to be 'Old Ho' (老 何). Courtesy of National Botanic Gardens, Glasnevin, Dublin.

Davidia involucrata, also known as the 'Handkerchief Tree'. Henry's rediscovery of this rare specimen helped make his reputation. Courtesy of Bette Cox.

E. H. Wilson's Chinese plant collectors, four of whom are said to have been trained by Henry to collect plants during the 1880s. Courtesy of the Arnold Arboretum Horticultural Library of Harvard University. © President and Fellows of Harvard College, Arnold Arboretum Archives.

Henry with Elsie in their Ranelagh garden in Dublin in the 1920s. The garden grew many of the plants that Henry had discovered in China. Courtesy of Dr Barbara Philips.

Terence MacSwiney. Courtesy of the National Library of Ireland.

Guo Moruo (in black, second from right) as a medical student in Kyushu, Japan, 1923. Courtesy of Guo Pingying.

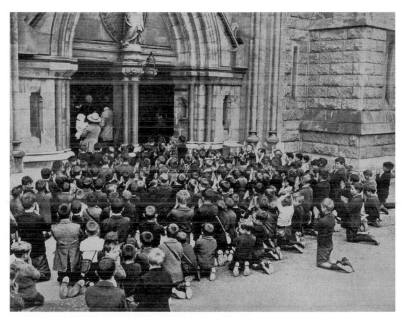

Schoolchildren praying for Terence MacSwiney, in front of Mary Immaculate Church, Inchicore, Dublin. Photograph is taken from *L'Illustration*, no. 4044, September 4, 1920. © Getty Images.

Lord Mayor of Cork MacSwiney's death made world headlines.

Terence MacSwiney's body lying in state in Southwark Catherdal

A photograph of MacSwiney lying in state, recirculated after the death of hunger striker Bobby Sands in 1981. Courtesy Bobby Sands Trust Archive.

Sketch for the Funeral of Terence MacSwiney, Lord Mayor of Cork 1920, by John Lavery, oil on canvas, 1920. Courtesy of Crawford Art Gallery Collection.

to the Augustine Henry Forestry Herbarium, compiled in the eight years after his death by his second wife, Alice. But one does not need to go to the Botanical Gardens in Dublin or even to Kew in London to see the treasures Henry brought from China. In the end, his most enduring legacy will be every one of the many plants bearing the specific epithet of Henry: *henryii, henryanus,* or *augustinii.* The glorious orange-gold lily that bears his name; the buddleia, which now grows wild even in our urban areas; the camellia; the blue-flowered *Rhododendron augustinii*; and the fragrant *Viburnum henryi:* these are Henry's most tangible legacy – as well as the many magnificent trees and amazing flowers that now adorn gardens, large and small, in Ireland and every other temperate zone of the Western world.

Endnotes

1   20 March 1885, Kew mss. 579. All other letters from Henry to directors at Kew Gardens are in this archive.

2   Seamus O'Brien (2011), *In the Footsteps of Augustine Henry and his Chinese Plant Collectors*, China: Garden Art Press, p. 22.

3   This is a society dedicated to the study of natural history, evolution and taxonomy. It was founded in 1778 by Botanist Sir James Edward Smith. It was called after Carolus Linnaeus, who systematized biological classification through his binomial nomenclature.

4   Emil Bretschneider (1898), *History of European Botanical Discoveries in China*, London: Sampson Lowe, Marston & Co., vol. 2, p. 775.

5   O'Brien (2011), p. 79.

6   Henry, Augustine (1902), 'Midst Chinese Forests,' *Garden* vol. 61, pp. 3–6. For the full quotation, see O'Brien (2011), pp. 84–85.

7   *Bulletin of Miscellaneous Information* (Kew Gardens publication, 1889). Abbreviated as *BMI* in following quotations.

8   The David of 'Plantae Davidiana' was in fact Père Jean Pierre Armand David who had supplied these 'novelties' based on his trip to China in 1862 while attached to the mission of the Lazarists at Beijing. From there he had explored much of the north of the country. In 1869, while travelling to Mupin (Boaxing) County in Szechuan (Sichuan) Province, he discovered – a first for Europeans – the Handkerchief Tree and the giant panda.

9   O'Brien (2011), p. 297.

10 Ibid., p. 313.

Staging the Revolution: Guo Moruo and Terence MacSwiney

Jerusha McCormack

On 12 August 1920, Terence MacSwiney was arrested for being a member of the Irish Republican Army by the forces of the British Crown in Cork: one of the leading cities in what was then a very restive part of the British Empire. Although the Irish insurrection had taken place four years previously, during Easter 1916, it had been deemed a military failure. In an effort to consolidate that revolutionary effort, the Irish Republican Army was engaged in a ferocious guerrilla war with British security forces seeking to maintain imperial control of the island.

On the day of MacSwiney's arrest, a young Chinese poet by the name of Guo Moruo, nominally a medical student in Kyushu, Japan, was in the throes of writing his first book of poetry. Born in 1892 during the last decades of the Qing dynasty, Guo was now, along with many Chinese intellectuals, living in self-imposed exile from a country that had descended into political chaos. Nevertheless, he was an ardent nationalist with a vision of what he saw as a future – and modernized – China. Along with others, Guo had been sent to Japan by the Chinese government to be trained in practical skills to help modernize China. Instead, prolonging his stay there, he became a founder of what was to become the Creation Society, generating a nexus of young men who saw their future roles as helping to create a new nation through a new way of writing.

While still in medical school in Japan, Guo Moruo was honing his writing skills working as a jobbing journalist. To follow the international news he needed to attend the telegraph office nearly every day. After the events of its abortive revolt in 1916, Ireland – like China, in political turmoil – had remained very much in the news. Thus it was, through a series of urgent telegrams telling of the arrest of Terence MacSwiney, that Guo first heard his name. From these dispatches, Guo may also have learned that Terence MacSwiney was, in many ways, pursuing a path parallel to his own. Like Guo, he was young, an idealist, a principled activist in the name of freedom. Unlike Guo, he was a politician. First elected for mid-Cork as a member of the new Dáil Éireann (the newly established Irish parliament), MacSwiney then took up a position in Cork County Council. In March 1920, following the assassination of his predecessor Tomás MacCurtain by British forces, he had been appointed Lord Mayor of Cork.

What MacSwiney shared with Guo was a belief in the power of the written word. In 1918, two years before his arrest, his slim book of poems, *Battle Cries*, was published. It was not, as expected, a lament for those fallen in the Great War but a call for heroes ready to die for Ireland. For, in common with Guo, MacSwiney clearly believed writing should be a form of propaganda. To provide a public platform for his passionate arguments, MacSwiney had founded a newspaper under the banner of *Fianna Fáil* [Irish for 'warriors of destiny']: *A Journal for Militant Ireland*. Suppressed in December 1914 after only eleven issues, due to its extreme republican and anti-British content, these editorials were published a year after MacSwiney's death under the title *Principles of Freedom* (1921).

What MacSwiney and Guo both understood was that independence did not mean merely a change of political regime but also a shift in the way people imagined their country. For MacSwiney, as for William Butler Yeats, literature could be an instrument for transforming the hearts and minds of the Irish people. Both men were also convinced that public drama would probably prove to be the most effective means of helping an emerging nation to imagine its future. To this end, Yeats and fellow spirits founded the Abbey as the national theatre in 1904. Following his lead, four years later MacSwiney set up the Cork Dramatic Society, for which he composed five plays. His last (called *The Revolutionist*, written three years before his arrest) was to provide MacSwiney with the script for his own final public performance as an Irish martyr.

For his own part, Guo Moruo was also, from exile, dramatizing himself publicly through his poetry as a romantic revolutionary. As did many of his Chinese contemporaries in Japan, Guo sought to import a new modernity for China by translating key Western texts. For Guo, this meant locating poetic – as well as political – models in the revolutionary poems of Percy Bysshe Shelley, Lord Byron and (above all) Walt Whitman. On the day Terence MacSwiney was arrested, Guo Moruo, already steeped in the language of romantic martyrdom, was primed poetically to embrace the particular fate lying in wait for MacSwiney.

Like MacSwiney, Moruo had come to understand that the prize here was not a heroic bloody death in battle but a battle for the hearts and minds of their fellow countrymen. Surprisingly, although MacSwiney was an ardent member of the Irish Republican Army, he did not believe in the efficacy of physical force. More effectual, as he came to see, was a kind of psychic jiu-jitsu by which the opposing force was used against itself. MacSwiney had faith that the political enemy, the British occupying force and the authorities behind them, still believed in those sterling British virtues of fair play and honour. He also recognized that the Irish were, as always in any contest with the forces of the British Empire, hopelessly outnumbered and outgunned. Thus the real battle, as he understood it, was one engaging not physical, but spiritual force. In the year he was arrested, MacSwiney articulated this belief in his inaugural address as Lord Mayor of Cork, in the sentences which were, in effect, to become his epitaph: 'This contest of ours is not on our side a rivalry of vengeance but one of endurance; it is not they who can inflict the most, but they who can suffer most who will conquer …'

MacSwiney's mode of resistance to his arrest was not novel; there had been deaths from hunger strikes (even recently) before his. But his suffering – due to its timing, its length and its value as sheer public spectacle – was to set an example that was to revolutionize the thinking of many freedom fighters to follow, such as Mahatma Ghandi and Nelson

Mandela. For MacSwiney was now about to enact his principles literally. Six days after he was arrested and transported to Brixton prison in London, on 16 August 1920, Terence MacSwiney went on hunger strike. He was to die slowly, painfully and very publicly over the next seventy-four days to intense national as well as international media attention.

Meanwhile, in faraway Japan, reading the telegraph dispatches relentlessly chronicling MacSwiney's decline as they came in, Guo Moruo began to piece them together into a poem. This poem became more than a journal; it became an event: an act that could transform its collective audience into a new spiritual community. If this is the essence of romantic nationalism, it was also, quite consciously, an act of propaganda as well. 'Literature,' Guo wrote later, 'should be a kind of revolutionary manifesto.'

But when this poem was finally published in his first book of poetry, *The Goddesses* (女神), a year after MacSwiney's death, it was not read merely as revolutionary propaganda – but as a poem that gave a voice to a new and powerful cultural revolution, reviving the fervour of China's own revolutionary moment in the famous May Fourth Movement two years previously. Today the poem may be taken as a cardinal example of how the literal can become the literary – and the literary the literal. It is exactly this convertibility that makes the two figures of MacSwiney and Guo so cognate. In such a context, MacSwiney's death could be seen as a kind of poetic propaganda in action; Guo's poem as an act of political incitement.

Guo Moruo's contemporaries were well aware of how literal and literary revolutions could often be so intertwined as, at times, to become transposable. In terms of the literal revolution, Ireland's long struggle for independence from Great Britain had, by 1920, already received considerable publicity among intellectuals in China. During the early twentieth century, journals such as *Short Story Monthly* (1910–), *The Eastern Miscellany* (1904–48) and *Literature Weekly* (1921–9) had already devoted special attention to Ireland. As noted by Chen Li:

> A search with 'Ireland' as the key word of the digitalized database of *The Eastern Miscellany* reveals more than eight hundred results, many focusing on the Irish political situation, with titles like 'Irish Home Rule' (by Zhang Xiechen [1912], vol. 9, no. 1), 'The Truth

of the Irish Rebellion' (by Xu Jiaqing [1916], vol. 13, no. 8) and 'The Historical Relationship between Ireland and Great Britain, and Their Negotiation Process' (by Yu Shixiu [1922], vol. 19, no.4).

From the following graph, one can see how in 1920, the year Guo published his poem, articles from *The Eastern Miscellany* with the key word 'Ireland' reached a peak before declining steeply.[1]

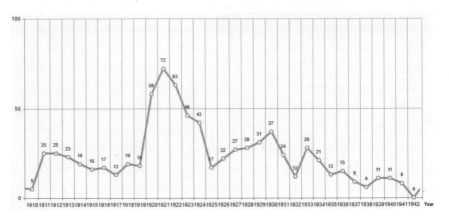

Mentions of 'Ireland' in *The Eastern Miscellany*, 1910–1948

In other words, Guo knew his audience. Ireland had become a popular model for revolution ever since the Russian Revolution in 1917, when Chinese intellectuals began to see the potential of Marxist theory. Although Guo Moruo was not to translate Marxist theorical texts until 1924, he would have known that Marx regarded the cause of Irish independence as part of the international struggle of the working class against the bourgeoisie. Marx's colleague Friedrich Engels, in particular, not only observed the tactics of resistance deployed by Irish workers in his father's cotton mill in Manchester but also learned a great deal about the Irish community there from the Irish woman who was to become his life-partner, Rosie Burns. So at that particular moment the idea of the Irish as model revolutionaries would have been vividly present in the minds of Chinese intellectuals, creating an audience eager for the news of the events of Easter 1916 as well as its aftermath in the Irish War of Independence – then being waged by proxy through the drama of MacSwiney's prolonged and very public death.

Literary Revolution Becomes Literal Revolution

Literal revolution came to China through a literary one. Those who sought to create a modern China knew that it could not be brought about through its own resources – it would need to be imported. Thus it became, as is generally recognized by Chinese scholars, a 'translated modernity'.[2] Disillusioned with traditional Chinese culture, intellectuals such as Guo Moruo and such contemporaries as Lu Xun (1881–1936) and Mao Dun (1896–1981) advocated turning to Western models. This meant importing key concepts such as 'science' and 'democracy' into the Chinese vocabulary as well as the literal translation of key texts. Among these were writings from the Irish literary revival, which in many ways ran parallel to China's own struggle to discover possible political and cultural solutions to China's own problems.

Initially these texts were not imported for their literary as much as for their political value: as powerful instruments for social change. W. B. Yeats in particular drew attention as an activist for the nationalist cause. For instance, as noted by Chen Li: 'In March 1920, *The Eastern Miscellany* (vol. 17, no. 6) published an important critical essay, "A Counter-Current in Contemporary Literature – New Writings in Ireland" by Yanbing (better known later as Mao Dun), together with his translation of W. B. Yeats's play *The Hour Glass* (1903)': certainly the earliest translation of any work by Yeats into Chinese.[3] More significant was its accompanying essay, in which Mao Dun, in the course of introducing Yeats as one of three leading dramatists of the Irish revival (the other two being Lady Gregory and J. M. Synge), summarizes what he called their 'counter-current' features: 'While [Chinese] people were questioning the future and favouring cosmopolitanism, the Irish were paying particular attention to their own history and national traits. The new Irish literature formed a unique school of its own.'[4]

Although he never attempted to translate Irish literary works, Guo Moruo had already refined his techniques on a set of three romantic revolutionary poets: Percy Bysshe Shelley (who wrote *Prometheus Unbound*, dramatizing a revolt against the gods); Lord Byron (whose dedication to the cause of freedom resulted in his death in the Greek War of Independence); and Walt Whitman (the poet of a new, democratic America). These poets – in particular Whitman – embodied a fervent revolutionary zeal. By translating them into the Chinese social/political scene during this period of cultural upheaval, Guo helped to authorize a Chinese modernity inextricable from interactions with the rest of the world. Thus, during the course of the poem he was in the very act of creating, Guo identified MacSwiney with freedom fighters not only from Ireland but also from Scotland and Poland, expressing an international solidarity with the 'countries of the weak and oppressed'.[5] In rendering their actions as radical poetry, theirs could also be read as a poetry of radical action.

So from the outset, Guo's finished poem on MacSwiney's fate, entitled 'Victorious in Death', features as one of China's first international poems (cited at the end of this essay). It was thus appropriately eclectic, even macaronic, quoting a minor Scottish poet (Thomas Campbell) in English, as if to underline its point. It was international in another sense, insofar as Guo cobbled it together from the telegrams about MacSwiney that he was following as a journalist. Their urgent staccato lines recreate this death as if in a sustained dramatic narrative. Thus, while honouring MacSwiney as an 'Irish patriot' and 'fighter for freedom', each verse, as drawn from daily telegraph dispatches, is dated, adding to its suspense. Will MacSwiney call off his hunger strike and live? Will the powers that govern the British Empire intervene? Or will they remain adamant in the face of this dramatic and very public challenge?

In the first verse, dated seven weeks after MacSwiney's arrest, Guo paints a picture of how, outside the 'gaunt forbidding pile' of Brixton prison in London where MacSwiney lies dying, 'A countless throng of young men kneel at prayer'. Imagining their prayers, the poet addresses the crowd directly:

Honoured MacSwiney!
Dear sons of Ireland,
the spirit of freedom will ever stand by you,
for you stand by one another,
you are the incarnation of freedom!

In the next verse, dated a little more than a week later, the poet asks, 'Are you still alive, locked in your prison cell?' Guessing that the end is near, the poet recalls an earlier report:

> Came a cable of the 17th from London:
> It was sixty-six days since your fast began,
> and yet you bear yourself as well as ever.
> You talked for a while with your dear ones on the afternoon of the 17th,
> and your face was even more radiant than before.

On that very day, Guo notes that Michael Fitzgerald, a fellow Corkman and comrade Sinn Féiner, had died after sixty-eight days on hunger strike. Fearing that MacSwiney will be next, he pairs him with Fitzgerald as two ancient lords of China (Po-yi and Shu-ch) who also starved to death as the result of a political protest – the only direct correlation with any Chinese events, mythical or otherwise, in the poem.

Sensing the tragedy is about to reach its climax, Guo ends the stanza: 'The next cable I dread to read …'. And the next is dreadful indeed:

> Now arrives a cable of the 21st:
> Three times MacSwiney has fainted.
> His sister has sent a telegram to his friends,
> hoping that the citizens have offered prayers for her brother.
> She prays that he may die the sooner, and his agony be ended.
> Who could bear to read to the end these heart-breaking words?
> Who could restrain his tears?

Reacting violently to the news, the poet denounces the 'Bestial murderous government' led by 'cruel, callous Englishmen': a sentiment that would resonate for its Chinese audience, who, to this day, recall as a 'century of humiliation' their defeat and ersatz colonialization after the two Opium Wars initiated by the British Empire. In the final stanza, written on 25 October 1920 – a day after the news of MacSwiney's death (aged 41) – Guo turns from lament to rhetorical exclamation:

> Brave, tragic death! Death in a blaze of glory! Triumphal procession of a
> victor! Victorious death!
> Impartial God of Death! I am grateful to you! You have saved MacSwiney
> for whom my love and reverence know no bounds!
> MacSwiney, fighter for freedom, you have shown how great can be the
> power of the human will!
> I am grateful to you, I extol you; freedom can henceforth never die!

When published under the title of *The Goddesses* a year later, in 1921, this poem, among others, created a literary sensation. No one in China had ever read poetry like this before. The Chinese tradition, never broken until now, was that of a very different kind of poetry. Composed within the formulas of classical Chinese, it tended to be formal in style, emotionally muted, heavily allusive. In its composition, everything was approached ceremoniously and sideways. Suddenly here was a poem exploding into the vernacular, not the expected classical Chinese, and addressing its readers directly – and not merely directly, but with a ferocious urgency. For its readers, such intensity must have felt like a full-frontal assault.

Also, breaking through centuries of tradition, its models were not the famous poets of China's long past but drawn from various international, particularly English, poets – and especially the great Romantic rebels, Shelley and Byron. From these Guo imported a new literary style of declamatory particles that tended to erupt in short outcries – followed by an exclamation mark. Few people in China had ever seen an exclamation mark or even an exclamatory particle in literature before.[6] A direct importation from the apostrophes of the Romantic poets of the West, its use marked a radical departure from traditional style, resulting in lines that were at once fragmented, informal and heavily demonstrative. Thus did one imported piece of punctuation (and its accompanying grammatical particle) dictate a drastic new poetics in which the old rigid forms of classical poetry collapsed into the informal flow of free verse, adapted in particular from Guo's translations of Whitman.

Guo first read Whitman in 1919, the year the May Fourth Movement broke out. It had, in fact, taken at least a year for him to realize how, through Whitman's poems, 'I came to see what to write and how to voice my personal troubles and the nation's suffering'.[7] Guo's dialectic of how self and society were shaping each other at this moment of revolutionary crisis is perhaps best articulated by the famous poet Wen Yiduo's remark that Guo articulated the 'suppressed emotions' of the young people of the May Fourth Movement in *The Goddesses* – thus rekindling what was becoming a fading force.[8] In Yidou's words, this 'really new' poetry was an 'historical breakthrough' and as such was hailed as a revolutionary act, driven by the 'rebellious spirit' of his age.[9] For these reasons, this first book of Guo's poetry has been credited, long after the fact, as encapsulating that 'deeper social change'[10] that led literary youths to become political youths: a shift from cultural to political nationalism that would find its parallel in the course of revolutionary Ireland.

Of course, not everything in Gou's early poetry was owed to his importation of foreign literary forms. Perhaps the most potent influence on Guo's poem about Terence MacSwiney was, in fact, the instrument of its composition: the electric telegraph. In transcribing its dispatches almost literally, Guo had wittingly become part of another global transaction: the mode of modern world media. From its transmissions, Guo appropriated the immediacy as well as the urgency we associate with the news – making it into a new voice by which a modern China could express itself to itself – and now to a world expanding exponentially by means of this new mechanical medium.

For it is thanks to the telegraph that, by the time *The Goddesses* was published more than a year after his death, MacSwiney's act had gained worldwide fame. As in Guo's case, the saga of MacSwiney's prolonged death had become the stuff of daily dispatches. Why and how did MacSwiney's death command such attention? First of all, because Ireland itself was acquiring a new voice through its writers, as already acknowledged by leading Chinese intellectuals. And that voice, like Guo's, was a dramatic one: in a literary sense, it was already staging the revolution. Four years before Terence MacSwiney founded the Cork Dramatic Society and more than a decade before he wrote *The Revolutionist* (1915), giving a platform and script for his actual role, W. B. Yeats had written two crucial plays for his new national theatre, the Abbey. There his *Cathleen ni Houlihan* (1902) famously dramatized the allegory of how a beautiful young Ireland sold her soul to the devil to buy her people freedom from famine. In Ireland, it had had such an effect on its public that Yeats was to ask, years later, 'Did that play of mine send out / Certain men the English shot?'[11] Closer in theme to the political drama of MacSwiney's death was Yeats's play *The King's Threshold* (1904), reviving an ancient Irish tale about a poet who made a show by starving himself at the king's door as a reproach for his overlord's treatment of him. Through such plays, composed for the Abbey Theatre as part of a greater nationalist project, the stage was literally being set for the larger, public performances of the Irish fight for freedom, such as that of MacSwiney's own martyrdom.

As a worldwide, expanding medium, the telegraph and its news outlets in the popular press were rapidly boosting the appetite of its audience for such public spectacles. Ireland is a small country still, with a modest population. Yet by 1920 the daily dispatches of the international press concerning MacSwiney's hunger strike would reach the millions of Irish and Irish descendants scattered throughout the world in a diaspora that reached from America to Argentina to China itself. Further, as a member of the then British Empire – still in the 1920s composing about a third of the world – news from Ireland would also reach its target audience in English in almost any part of its domain, from India to Africa or Australia to Canada. That huge reading public, largely Christian, would also have recognized in the death of MacSwiney another drama: that of the public death of Jesus of Nazareth. Interpreted as heroic martyrdom, such a death is seen as the ultimate sacrifice one might make for a set of beliefs – so valuable in themselves that, without them, life has no meaning. Terence MacSwiney lived, and died, a devout Roman Catholic. Although now known only as a specific sect of Christianity, Roman Catholicism is itself a world Church, with vast congregations in many countries throughout the globe. Its media had and still retains, through its global networks, an efficient way of transmitting news to a receptive audience. In MacSwiney's case, what would have been transmitted is the way that political drama was being re-enacted as a spiritual – and specifically Christian – one. In his inaugural speech as

Lord Mayor of Cork, MacSwiney's rhetoric sealed this identification, asserting that 'Spiritual liberty … comes to us dripping in the Blood of Christ Crucified.'[12]

Indeed, the recent Irish insurrection directly invoked that same model in being deliberately planned and executed (that is the right word) on Easter Monday 1916 – just four years before MacSwiney's own death. Why Easter Monday? As every Irish person knows, the day following Easter is a public holiday – originally declared by the British and still a part of today's Irish holiday calendar. As a non-working day, all the main controlling forces of the British Empire in Ireland would not have been at their desks. Thus a perfect day for a popular uprising. But more importantly, it invoked the model of Jesus of Nazareth's heroic martyrdom, not merely as a symbolic sacrifice for a set of beliefs – but also as a triumphant sacrifice, according to the Christian belief that Jesus of Nazareth did not in fact die but was resurrected from the dead.

Not only the timing was heavily symbolic. Those taking part in what is called the Easter Rising also knew on some level they had to fail – and their lives be sacrificed – as they were in fact (as MacSwiney pointed out in his inaugural address) both outnumbered and outgunned. But what Terence MacSwiney understood was how (in his own words) 'a seeming defeat may be a real victory. The Rebellion of 1916 is a case in point … The Rebellion was a success.'[13] It was a logic at the heart of the Irish nationalist movement. Where physical force failed, spiritual force would triumph, if only through the Christian logic in which heroic failure ultimately becomes triumphant victory.

That same transformation is chronicled in one of W. B. Yeats's great revolutionary poems, 'Easter 1916'. In retelling its course, Yeats uses the metaphor of public theatre, describing the personae involved as if they were actors in a play. What the poem chronicles is just how these actors were transformed from 'jesters' or apparent clowns, the subject of private jokes, into heroes for the cause of Irish independence. The catalyst for such transformation was their martyrdom at the hands of the British authorities who, over the course of nine days, executed the fifteen imprisoned freedom fighters one by one. During this crucial period, the Irish public, at first largely annoyed by, or indifferent to, the disruption caused by the Easter Rising, were riveted by this public drama, in particular because it involved not professional soldiers but writers who were idealists and dreamers caught up in the brutal machinery of the British Empire. Chronicling this dramatic conversion, the last line of the poem still resonates as its epitaph: 'A terrible beauty is born'.

Beauty born from terror could also describe the world's reaction to the agonized but very public dying of Terence MacSwiney. Sensing the public reaction, Yeats first published the poem 'Easter 1916' in the *New Statesman* just two days *before* MacSwiney died – although it was actually written just after the events of Easter 1916 nearly four years earlier. It was a calculated as well as brilliantly timed move. As was Yeats's next decision, only four months after MacSwiney's death, to stage his play *The Revolutionist* at the Abbey Theatre. Produced at a moment when the national theatre's finances were in poor shape, this publicity coup led to such a successful run that the finances more than recovered for the first time in many months.[14] As if to seal the theatrical metaphor, nearly a year after MacSwiney's death Yeats rewrote his early play *The King's Threshold*, giving it a new and more tragic ending where, instead of a moral triumph over his lord, the fasting poet dies as a result of the king's intransigence.

Meanwhile, the larger drama following MacSwiney's death had already seized centre stage. Over centuries of opposition to the British Empire, the Irish had learned that one of the most effective modes of protest on the death of a nationalist figure was a large and very public funeral. Funerals still remain key public events in Ireland. In the case of a freedom fighter such as MacSwiney, the rituals of the Roman Catholic Church would once again enact the adamant faith of the common Irish people that had supported them during such catastrophes as the Great Famine in the late 1840s: an event evoked by MacSwiney's own decision to refuse food as the only weapon of defiance left to him against what he saw as the British oppressor. Although the British authorities tried to represent his death as a kind of suicide, MacSwiney himself was clear that he was acting as a soldier prepared to die for a cause – as part of a campaign to bring to the attention of the world the cause of Irish freedom. As a devout Catholic, he would have done so believing in the Christian promise that his spirit would not die but become immortal.

Given all these symbolic resonances, the British authorities rightly feared public unrest at MacSwiney's funeral. But faced with the Roman Catholic authorities, in particular the formidable Bishop of Southwark in London, the British establishment backed down. Accordingly there followed an elaborate funeral at Southwark Cathedral – actually commemorated in a painting by the Irish artist (knighted by the British) Sir John Lavery. Although a funeral (but not a procession) was forbidden in Dublin out of fear of political unrest, a second, even larger church service followed in MacSwiney's hometown of Cork. This was deemed by the press to be of such worldwide interest that it was actually filmed. Excerpts can still be found on YouTube today.[15]

Just as news of MacSwiney's prolonged fast had reached Guo Moruo through the electric telegraph, it now played a leading part in transmitting news of his death and two funerals to a worldwide media platform. The press's detailed reports – along with vivid photographs of every stage of the rituals – through the lying in state of MacSwiney's body to the funeral processions through London, Dublin and, finally, Cork and subsequent obsequies – culminated in a long series of news dispatches. During the seventy-four days he took to die, MacSwiney's fast had already gathered prolonged media attention in Europe (especially Paris and Rome), sometimes on a daily basis. As he lay dying, British newspapers began to demand government action. Once his death was announced, members of trade unions in New York city refused to unload British cargo ships. Protests are recorded to have taken place in India, Brazil and Spain (where the Catalan Trade Union held strikes in sympathy). The role of the press in dramatizing MacSwiney's death may be gauged by the headlines of one Italian paper that reads in large bold print: 'MacSwiney's agony ... Long Live the Republic of Ireland!' But it was the *New York Times* that found exactly the right metaphor when it described MacSwiney's fast to the death as 'a gesture of deep tragedy on a stage where all mankind looks on'.

In terms of outcomes, the death of Terence MacSwiney amounted to more than a passing tabloid sensation. In the United

Kingdom, towards the end of the hunger strike, King George V had stated in a telegram to Prime Minister Lloyd George: 'Were he to be allowed to die in prison, results would be deplorable. His Majesty would be prepared to exercise clemency if you could so advise and believes that this would be a wise course.' Although that 'wise course' was not followed, MacSwiney's hunger strike commanded a good deal of liberal sympathy even within the United Kingdom, with the *Daily Telegraph* commenting within a day of his death (26 October 1920) that 'The Lord Mayor condemned himself to death for the sake of a cause in which he passionately believed, and it is impossible for men of decent instincts to think of such an act unmoved.' Yet even while expressing sympathy with his act, it was condemned as 'an unfair weapon [as] an attempt to coerce by lacerating the feelings of one's adversary'.

Such psychic jiu-jitsu left many in authority with similarly divided minds. Yet, within weeks of MacSwiney's death, the first tentative discussions about peace between Irish representatives and the British government were taking place in the Foreign Office in London. In China, almost as if in a parallel universe, Guo Moruo's electrifying poem on MacSwiney, 'Victorious in Death', galvanized the youth of the May Fourth Movement into new political momentum. Further afield, among the Chinese overseas, it is said to have helped create a new, imagined community of those seeking to create a new, modernized China: among them Zhou Enlai and Deng Xiaoping – students in Paris – as well as the many Chinese intellectuals, comrades of Guo Moruo, studying in Japan. In effect, what the poem 'Victorious in Death' does, within the larger context of *The Goddesses*, is to validate a 'universal' revolutionary fervour – one not merely nationalistic but transnational – as a kind of spiritual life force.

In so doing, 'Victorious in Death' also created a newly revolutionary kind of poetry, employing a rhetoric both self-empowering and self-cancelling. Through its words, the poet fashions himself into an instrument transmitting that passionate, public voice that would seek to transform its world. Enacting his own rhetoric, MacSwiney too sought to become an instrument for the cause of Irish independence. Inspired by his death, in London a young Ho Chi Minh, future founder of the Democratic Republic of Vietnam, is said to have exclaimed: 'A nation which has such citizens will never surrender.' When published a year after his death, MacSwiney's book, *Principles of Freedom*, translated into a number of Indian languages, is reported to have had a profound influence on Mahatma Gandhi and Jawaharlal Nehru. Faced with his own execution in 1931, the Indian anti-colonialist Bhagat Singh quoted MacSwiney, saying, 'I am confident that my death will do more to smash the British Empire than my release.'

In Ireland, up to quite recently, hunger strikes still served to play a powerful role in the Irish Republican Army's political resistance to British rule in Northern Ireland (the most recent example being the deaths by hunger of Bobbie Sands along with nine other inmates of the Maze/Long Kesh Prison who fasted to death in 1981). But none co-opted the world stage in the same way as that of Terence MacSwiney. Not only do the older people in Ireland today recognize the importance of his death, among the young the memory is kept fresh in media such as the wall paintings at a local Gaelic Athletic Association sports ground – or the one that features the face of a young Palestinian inscribed with his words: 'It is not those who can inflict but those that can suffer the most who will conquer.' Words that serve to remind us that Terence MacSwiney did not die only for Irish freedom nor even for a more universal political freedom – but for what he saw as the spiritual freedom of oppressed peoples – in all places and for his time – and ours.

Victorious in Death

I.

Oh! once again to Freedom's cause return,
The patriot Tell – the Bruce of Bannockburn!
'True depiction of 'the sea of tears,'
gaunt forbidding pile: can it be the gateway to a prison, or the outside of a church?
A countless throng of young men kneel at prayer.
'MacSwiney, leader of the Irish Republican Army,
cast into Parkstone Gaol fifty days ago and more,
has spurned ever since the shameful English bread.

We sons of Ireland, kneeling before this great building,
are deeply moved by his devotion.
We offer up our prayers for his protection.'

Honoured MacSwiney!
Dear sons of Ireland,
the spirit of freedom will ever stand by you,
for you stand by one another,
you are the incarnation of freedom!

October 13

II.

Hope, for a season, bade the world farewell,
And Freedom shrieked – as Kosciusko fell!
Terence MacSwiney, Irish patriot!
Today is the 22nd of October!
(Never has the calendar on the wall so fixed my attention!)
Are you still alive, locked in your prison cell?
Came a cable of the 17th from London:
It was sixty-six days since your fast began,
and yet you bear yourself as well as ever.
You talked for a while with your dear ones on the afternoon of the 17th,
and your face was even more radiant than before.
Your strength was fading daily …
and today is the 22nd of October.
Irish patriot, Terence MacSwiney!
Can you still be counted among living creatures?
A cable of the 17th from your native Cork
told that a Sinn Feiner, a comrade of yours, Fitzgerald,
fasted for sixty-eight days in Cork City Gaol,
and suddenly died at sundown on the 17th.
Cruel deaths there are in history, but few so tragic.
The Shouyang Mountain of Ireland! The Po-yi and Shu-chi of Ireland!
The next cable I dread to read …

October 22

III.

O sacred Truth! Thy triumph ceased awhile,
And Hope, thy sister, ceased with thee to smile.
Now arrives a cable of the 21st:
Three times MacSwiney has fainted.
His sister has sent a telegram to his friends,
hoping that the citizens have offered prayers for her brother.
She prays that he may die the sooner, and his agony be ended.
Who could bear to read to the end these heart-breaking words?
　　　Who could restrain his tears?
Bestial murderous government, are you bent on casting
　　　an indelible stain on the history of the world?
Cruel, callous Englishmen, has the blood of Byron and Campbell
　　　ceased to flow in your veins?
Lustreless moon, would that our sombre earth might on the instant
be turned like you to ice!
　　　　　　October 24

IV.

Truth shall restore the light by Nature given,
And, like Prometheus, bring the fire of Heaven!
The mighty ocean is sobbing its sad lament,
the boundless abyss of the sky is red with weeping,
far, far away the sun has sunk in the west.
Brave, tragic death! Death in a blaze of glory! Triumphal procession of a
　　　victor! Victorious death!
Impartial God of Death! I am grateful to you! You have saved MacSwiney
　　　for whom my love and reverence know no bounds!
MacSwiney, fighter for freedom, you have shown how great can be the
　　　power of the human will!
I am grateful to you, I extol you; freedom can henceforth never die!
The night has closed down on us, but how bright is the moon …
　　　　　　October 27

Guo Moruo (2001), *The Goddesses*, trans. Jong Lester and A. C. Barnes, Beijing: Foreign Languages Press, pp. 131–41.

《胜利的死》 – 作品原文

作者：郭沫若

爱尔兰独立军领袖，新芬党员马克司威尼，自八月中旬为英政府所逮捕以来，幽囚于剥里克士通监狱中，耻不食英粟者七十有三日，终以一千九百二十年十月二十五日死于狱。

其一

Oh! Once again to Freedom's cause return,
The patriot Tell – the Bruce of Bannockburn!
爱国者兑尔 – – 邦诺克白村的布鲁士①，
哦，请为自由之故而再生！

– – Thomas Campbell

哦哦！这是张"眼泪之海"的写真呀！
森严阴耸的大厦 – – 可是监狱的门前？可是礼拜堂的外面？
一群不可数尽的儿童正在跪着祈祷呀！

"爱尔兰独立军的领袖马克司威尼，
投在英格兰，剥里克士通监狱中已经五十余日了，
入狱以来耻不食英粟；
爱尔兰的儿童 – – 跪在大厦前面的儿童
感谢他爱国的至诚，
正在为他请求加护，祈祷。"

可敬的马克司威尼呀！
可爱的爱尔兰的儿童呀！
自由之神终会要加护你们，
因为你们能自相加护，
因为你们是自由神的化身故！

10月13日

其二

Hope, for a season, bade the world farewell,
And Freedom shrieked - as Kosciuszko fell!
希望，暂时向世界告别了，
自由也发出惊叫 - - 当珂斯修士哥死了！
- - Thomas Campbell

爱尔兰的志士！马克司威尼！
今天是十月二十二日了！（我壁上的日历永不曾引我如此注意）
你囚在剥里克士通监狱中可还活着在吗？
十月十七日伦敦发来的电信
说你断食以来已经六十六日了，
然而容态依然良好；
说你十七日的午后还和你的亲人对谈了须臾，
然而你的神采比从前更加光辉；
说你身体虽日渐衰颓，
然而今天是十月二十二日了！
爱尔兰的志士！马克司威尼呀！
此时此刻的有机物汇当中可还有你的生命存在吗？
十月十七日你的故乡 - - 可尔克市 - - 发来的电信
说是你的同志新芬党员之一人，匪持谢乐德，
因在可尔克市监狱中断食以来已六十有八日，
终以十七日之黄昏溘然长逝了。
　- - 啊！有史以来罕曾有的哀烈的惨死呀！
爱尔兰的首阳山！爱尔兰的伯夷，叔齐哟！
我怕读得今日以后再来的电信了！
10月22日

其三

Oh! sacred Truth! thy triumph ceased a while,
And Hope, thy sister, ceased with thee to smile.
哦，神圣的真理！你的胜利暂停了一忽，
你的姊妹，希望，也同你一道停止了微笑。
- - Thomas Campbell

十月二十一日伦敦发来的电信又到了！
说是马克司威尼已经昏死了去三回了！
说是他的妹子向他的友人打了个电报：
望可尔克的市民早为她的哥哥祈祷，
祈祷他早一刻死亡，少一刻痛伤！
不忍卒读的伤心人语哟！读了这句话的人有不流眼泪的吗？
猛兽一样的杀人政府哟！你总要在世界史中添出一个永远不能
磨灭的污点！
冷酷如铁的英人们呀！你们的血管之中早没有拜伦、康沫儿的
血液循环了吗？
你暗淡无光的月轮哟！我希望我们这阴莽莽的地球，
就在这一刹那间，早早同你一样冰化！
10月24日

其四
Truth shall restore the light by Nature given,
And, like Prometheus, bring the fire of Heaven!
真理，你将恢复自然所给予的光，
如像普罗美修士带来天火一样！
– –Thomas Campbell

汪洋的大海正在唱着他悲壮的哀歌，
穹窿无际的青天已经哭红了他的脸面，
远远的西方，太阳沉没了！－－
悲壮的死哟！金光灿烂的死哟！凯旋同等的死哟！
胜利的死哟！
兼爱无私的死神！我感谢你哟！你把我敬爱无暨的马克司威尼
早早救了！
自由的战士，马克司威尼，你表示出我们人类意志的权威如此
伟大！
我感谢你呀！赞美你呀！"自由"从此不死了！
夜幕闭了后的月轮哟！何等光明
呀！……
10月27日

Endnotes

1   Chen Li (2019), 'An Emerging Field: Irish Studies in China', *The Irish and China: Encounters and Exchanges*, Dublin: New Island, p. 114. The accompanying graph is from Chen Li (2018), 'Irish Literature in China', *Éire-Ireland*, vol. 53, nos. 3 & 4, pp. 273, 274.

2   For an in-depth study of Guo Moruo's role in this new modernity, see Pu Wang (2018), *The Translatability of Revolution: Guo Moruo and Twentieth-Century Chinese Culture*, Cambridge, MA: Harvard University Press – to which this essay is indebted.

3   Chen Li (2018), p. 273.

4   Jerusha McCormack (2013), 'Irish Studies in China: The Widening Gyre,' *Studi Irlandesi*, no. 3, pp. 157–80.

5   Wang, p. 55.

6   On Guo's 'linguistic radicalism' see Johannes Daniel Kaminski, 'Punctuation, Exclamation and Tears: *The Sorrows of Young Werther* in Japanese and Chinese Translation (1889–1922),' *Comparative Critical Studies*, vol. 14 no. 1, pp. 29–48 (accessed online May 2017). In this article, Kaminski remarks that 'Western punctuation had barely been introduced at the time.'

7   Liu Rongqian (2002), 'Whitman's Soul in China: Guo Moruo's poetry in the New Culture Movement,' in *Whitman East and West*, ed. Ed Folsom, Iowa City: University of Iowa Press.

8   *Over One Hundred Comments on Guo Moruo* (1992), eds Wang Jinhou, Qin Chuan, Tang Mingzhong, and Xiao Binru. Chengdu: Chengdu Publishing House, pp. 50–51 quoted in. Liu (2002), p. 183.

9   Ibid., p.184.

10 'Guo Moruo and the Chinese Revolution: A Review of *The Phenomenology of "Zeitgeist": Guo Moruo and the Chinese Revolution* by Pu Wang' (28 May 2015) from http://dissertationreviews.org/east-south-and-southeast-asia/chinese-literature (accessed 25 January 2018).

11 From his late poem 'The Man and the Echo' (1938).

12 From his inaugural address as Lord Mayor of Cork on 20 March 1920, included as an appendix to Máire MacSwiney Brugha (2005), *History's Daughter: A Memoir from the Only Child of Terence MacSwiney*, Dublin: O'Brien Press. Benedict Anderson, in his *Imagined Communities: Reflections on the Origin and Spread of Nationalism* (1983), has some potent observations on the necessity of blood sacrifice in sealing the social contract involved in creating a nation.

13 Toirdhealbhach Mac Suibhne [Terence MacSwiney] (1918). 'Appendix II', *The Ethics of Revolt. A Discussion from a Catholic Point of View as to When it Becomes Lawful to Rise in Revolt against the Civil Power.* Reprinted from *Irish Freedom*. Cork, p. 24.

14 Anthony Bradley (2009), 'Nation, Pedagogy, and Performance: W. B. Yeats's *The King's Threshold* and the Irish Hunger Strikes,' *Literature and History*, vol. 18, no. 2, p.26.

15 See https://www.youtube.com/watch?v=qU16rhRHP7M.

Bringing a Chinese Heaven to Irish Skies: Professor Tao Kiang

Luke Drury and Anna-Sophia Kiang

In developing the relationship between China, Ireland and the international astronomical community, Professor Tao Kiang (as he was known in his adopted country of Ireland) was a most remarkable individual. Perhaps because he worked mainly as a facilitator, keeping to the background, today the importance of his work is not as well recognized as it deserves to be. This essay is an attempt to redress the balance – as well as to honour the memory of a man who was as much at home in the culture of his native China as in that of the European Enlightenment: a true citizen of the world and a distinguished scientist in his own right. Only now is it possible to clarify how much his Chinese origins contributed to his Irish work in suggesting how astronomical calculations could be refined according to ancient Chinese observations of the heavens.

Born as Jiang Tao ('Great Wave of River') in Yangzhou, China, on 6 February 1929, Tao's parents were a progressive couple of the recently emerged Republic of China. His father, Jiang Zhen Guang, became a successful artist in the traditional watercolour style; greatly revered in his native Yangzhou, he was also renowned throughout Jiangsu province and beyond. Tao's mother, Wang Xin Ru, was similarly accomplished, having been raised within an enlightened family environment in which education was all-important for daughters as well as sons. She worked as a schoolteacher and did not have bound feet: both features exemplifying her pioneering spirit as well as the progressive attitude of her family. Tao had one elder sister, two younger brothers and a younger sister. The family residence was of the traditional four-sectioned compound style, with a central square courtyard garden enclosed by four one-storey buildings facing north, south, east, or west. By all reports, Tao's early childhood was a happy one – despite the obvious pressure on him to achieve greatness, being the eldest son of this high-achieving couple. Thus while his siblings attended local schools, Tao was sent, at an early age, to an elite boarding school in nearby Nanjing. There he flourished, excelling academically in mathematics, English, Chinese literature and calligraphy, as well as enjoying music, athletics and tai chi, among other subjects.

However, school life and idyllic family holidays in Yangzhou were rudely interrupted in 1937 when, during the Second Sino-Japanese war, the Japanese advanced towards Nanjing (a mere 96 kilometres south of Yangzhou). With the help of Tao's uncle, Jiang Xi-Lin, a diplomat working for Generalissimo Chiang Kai-Shek of the ruling Kuomintang Nationalist Party, the Jiang family fled the city amid rumours of unspeakable atrocities being committed against their fellow countrymen, eventually finding refuge in the countryside. Later that year they returned to their city dwelling. But during the ensuing two years, their relatively peaceful life again came under pressure, this time due to civil strife between the ruling Kuomintang and revolutionary Communist factions, which ultimately were to split up the family.

By this time, in 1939, it was decided that Tao should pretend to be his uncle's son. In this way, he could escape – along with his uncle, aunt and cousin – the worst of the turmoil in China by relocating to the suburbs of Chongqing, then the provisional capital of the Republic of China. This meant saying goodbye to his parents and siblings at the age of 10, as Chongqing, nearly 1,500 kilometres to the south-west of Yangzhou, was a distance few could cover in those days. Indeed, during their four-month journey to the Kuomintang capital, Tao and his adoptive family had many adventures: including being held up by bandits – from whom they managed to escape minus a few belongings. Once settled into a modest home outside the capital, Tao was again sent to boarding schools where he continued to excel in a diverse range of subjects.

Several years later Tao's fate took another turn when his uncle, Jiang Xi-Lin, having risen in the ranks of the diplomatic corps of the Kuomintang, was offered a post as cultural attaché to the Chinese ambassador to France. Thus in 1945, at the tender age of 16, Tao bade his motherland farewell and embarked on what was to be the beginning of the rest of his life. He could not know then that he would never again live in China nor that communications between him and his real family would prove impossible for nearly two decades.

One of Tao's first impressions of the West was watching the huge celebrations marking VE Day, on 8 May 1945, from his privileged dwelling along the Champs-Élysées where he enjoyed private tuition with emphasis on French and English. Meanwhile, back home, as the civil war intensified and the Kuomintang began to lose ground to the Communists in the late 1940s, Tao's family began to entertain siding with the revolutionaries – partly in an effort to survive and partly due to genuine sympathy with their cause. At about the same time, Jiang Xi-Lin was posted to Haiti and then subsequently retreated to Taiwan following the fall of the Kuomintang in China. Tao, on the other hand, aged only 20 and without financial backing (his uncle's income having been severely cut), decided to leave for London.

For a young Chinese man with neither connections nor money, life in London in the late 1940s was certainly challenging. However Tao's resilience – together with his ability to work hard at any job however menial – stood him in good stead. He took up lodgings in the YMCA and found casual jobs. At the same time, his thirst for knowledge never having diminished, he embarked upon night study, supporting himself by washing dishes in local restaurants by day. Ever ambitious, he first chose to study English literature – despite English being only his second (or maybe third) language at that time. It was during this time that he met and married a fellow student, Chen Xiao Ying – though perhaps more out of loneliness and a desire for a Chinese companion rather than out of pure love. For despite the birth of a daughter, Rosalind, in 1951, the marriage did not succeed. By now Tao had also long abandoned his literature degree course to embark upon another of his passions, music, teaching himself how to play both recorder and piano. If he soon realized that a musician's life was also not for him, throughout his life he played piano most days purely for the love of it. (In fact, his eightieth birthday present to himself was a brand new piano!)

Finally Tao turned his attention to the study of mathematics, obtaining a BSc from Birkbeck College, University of London, in the early 1950s. As his interest in astronomy was a natural progression from pure mathematics, he gladly seized the opportunity to become a research assistant to Professor C. W. Allen in Mill Hill Observatory, London University. Initially his employment there was as a 'plate reader', which involved categorizing and analyzing data obtained from photographs of the night sky captured on glass plates. Outside of work, Tao's wide-ranging interests and open-mindedness meant that he had many friends from all walks of life. So it happened that in 1957, during a retreat organized by the Theosophical Society, he met Trudi Kaczmarek, a young woman of Swiss extraction. They were married a year later, in their best clothes – their Polish dancing costumes – in what was to be a lifelong commitment ended only by Tao's death. Together they had four children: Ingmar, Sophie, Tanya and Jessica.

During these early married years, under the supervision of Professor Allen, Tao was encouraged to conduct his own research, which culminated in a thesis entitled 'Statistical Analyses of Asteroids and Galaxies' for which he was awarded a PhD in 1965. A year earlier, in 1964 – nineteen years after leaving China as a teenager – Tao returned there. During almost this whole time away, as he had been branded as a 'Kuomintang traitor', he had no way of communicating with his family. Now finally allowed back into China, Tao was overjoyed to be reunited with his family whom – having left aged 9 – he had not seen for twenty-five years. Like a thunderbolt, the words of Tao's favourite poet, He Zhi Zhang, from 'On Returning to My Hometown' came to him:

I left home a boy, I now return an old man,
My accent has not changed,
but hairs on my temples are in decline.
A child meets me, but recognizes me not,
Smiling, he asks, 'Sir, Where are you from?'

Tao recalled he was pleased that his family seemed well fed and healthy despite their lack of material possessions. He was also pleasantly surprised by how well the commune system appeared to be working – and of the general cleanliness of the city of Yangzhou. Thus he came back to London very upbeat about Communist China. But soon this optimism was dashed by reports of horrendous cruelty (especially towards academics such as his own family), events culminating in the Cultural Revolution that lasted over the decade from 1966–76. During this time, Tao was denied access to China; he was not to return until after the death of Mao in 1977.

Back home and at work, Tao pursued wide-ranging scientific interests. His first published paper (from 1955) had been an interesting study of whether the observed colours of B stars could be related to extinction by dust lanes and the spiral structure of our own galaxy (the absorption of light by interstellar dust causes the stars to appear redder in much the same way as the sun appears redder at sunrise and sunset). During this period at Mill Hill Observatory, Tao also published on the reduction of parallax measurements, asteroid counts, the luminosity distribution of galaxies (which involved some advanced statistical discussion of biases and incompleteness), the effect of a resisting medium on elliptical orbits and the distribution of ridges on the lunar surface.

Indeed, Tao's most cited work dates from this very fruitful period. Entitled 'Random Fragmentation in Two and Three Dimensions', it is noteworthy for using a very early computational simulation. In essence, the paper discusses how large the resulting 'chunks' are if space is divided up to follow the distribution of randomly distributed centres (technically using the Voronoi tessellation where each 'chunk' is just the set of points that are closer to a given centre than to any other). Tao was thinking of the distribution of galaxies and stars; but the mathematical problem is a general one of wide interest in many fields. Although this work was carried out while Tao was still in London, it was published only after his move to Dublin.

It was undoubtedly this wide range of interests, as well as his clear aptitude for mathematical and statistical analysis, that attracted Patrick Wayman, the recently appointed director of Dunsink Observatory in Dublin. Initially, however, Dublin was a second choice. Having established himself as a young astronomer of some note (with a particular interest in statistical analyses), Tao was soon offered several interesting career options. Notable among them in the mid-60s was a position in the astronomy department of Yale University in the US. But fate and politics again intervened, erecting an insurmountable barrier to this American dream. A few months earlier Tao, while out socializing with friends, had happened upon a meeting of a fledgling Communist group. Although Tao still loved China, he was ambivalent about Communism, the ideology of which had split up his family and cut him off from them for so long. Now once again it was putting them under renewed hardship due to the harsh policies of the Gang of Four. But in the era of McCarthyism, the US Embassy in London, having been informed of Tao's presence at that gathering, refused to issue him and his family with visas. It was at this point that fate again intervened, bringing him to Dunsink Observatory and Ireland. There he was to spend the rest of his life.

Constructed by Trinity College Dublin, Dunsink Observatory had been in operation since 1785. Its main claim to fame was the stellar reputation of the third director, Sir William Rowan Hamilton (1805–65) – undoubtedly the greatest mathematician and theoretical physicist that Ireland has ever produced, as well as a man who, even in his own day, enjoyed a global reputation. Hamilton was an iconic figure for the Irish politician and statesman Eamon de Valera, who himself very nearly became a mathematics lecturer in University College Cork and who, all his life, retained a genuine interest in mathematics. It was this admiration for Hamilton that led to de Valera's establishing the Dublin Institute for Advanced Studies in 1940. In 1947, after de Valera expanded the Institute by adding a School of Cosmic Physics, the Irish state purchased Dunsink Observatory from Trinity College to form part of the new school.

In 1964, when Patrick Wayman was appointed Head of Astronomy and Director of Dunsink, he immediately set about recruiting a second in command. In the process of consulting friends and colleagues, Tao's London mentor, Professor Allen, recommended Tao Kiang as a promising young astronomer whose broad theoretical interests would complement the more practical interests of the new director of Dunsink.

Appointed as Professor in 1966, Tao arrived that summer with Trudi and three children under the age of eight. Luckily, the job came with the use at nominal rent of Dunsink House, a fine four-bedroomed Victorian house on the grounds of the observatory that Trudi, ever creative, made into a comfortable family home. Altogether there were four families living on the Dunsink estate. The Director, Professor Patrick Wayman and his family occupied half of the main historic observatory building (the other half was the working observatory). The groundsman, Tom McDermot, and his family lived at the gate lodge; while technician Robin Murphy's family lived just beyond the eastern boundary. This small community ensured that Tao's children had ample playmates with which to share such a spacious playground.

At Dunsink, Tao enjoyed a happy family life, interrupted only occasionally by his disappointment that his children would rather play football or build camps than study Chinese, or that their school marks in history exceeded those for mathematics. In addition to his love of music (he often held chamber music soirées at home), Tao loved to dance. Magical summer evenings were spent with friends and family out on the main observatory green, Tao teaching Balkan, Greek, Israeli and Scottish dancing to the tunes and rhythms of carefully selected records. If the weather turned inclement, the dancing would simply continue in the observatory's dome in circular form around the telescope!

These early years at Dunsink were followed by a series of relocations: the first of these when, five years later, Tao and Trudi bought a brand new house in Deerpark, Castleknock. Then, for the academic year of 1973–4, the Kiang family all moved to Glasgow, where Tao had requested a sabbatical at the university. A year after their return to Ireland, Tao's youngest daughter, Jessica, was born – a welcome relief to him (no doubt), as he had been struggling a bit with his very Westernized other three, now pre-teens and teens, who did not always live up to his deep-seated Chinese ideals based on filial respect and obedience.

Since restrictions imposed on academics by the Communist Party were beginning to ease about this time (towards the end of the Cultural Revolution), Tao embarked upon setting up closer ties with Chinese astronomers. When he at last managed to get back into

China in 1977 to visit his family, he was dismayed to see how old and frail his parents had become – and how psychologically scarred some of his siblings and wider family members appeared. He vowed to return regularly and with as many gifts (including TV sets and other 'luxuries') as he could carry.

It is a tribute to Tao that, in addition to this intense family reunion, he also found time during this visit to set up formal links between Chinese universities and Dunsink Observatory, enabling students to travel to Ireland to undertake part of their doctoral research. Thus in the late 70s and throughout the 80s, Tao and Trudi began welcoming Chinese PhD-student astronomers into their home – some staying on for years. Many were well into their thirties or forties, for they had missed out on the opportunity to study in their younger years due to Chinese political diktats.

Tao's efforts as a cultural ambassador did not end here. Also during the 1977 visit, Tao worked to forge new links between You Xie, the Chinese Friendship Society and the Irish Chinese Cultural Society (ICCS): a group he and a few Irish friends had co-founded in 1975 to promote understanding between Ireland and China. As a result of these links, the Chinese government issued a formal invitation for the first delegation of 'ordinary' Irish people to visit China. Thus, in 1980, ten members of the ICCS, including Tao and Trudi, were treated to a five-star tour of China, visiting many cultural attractions – such as the Forbidden City in Beijing, the gardens of Suzhou and the famous mountains of Guilin to mention just a few. They were also given a formal audience in the Great Hall of the People, Tiananmen Square: a huge honour and one of Tao's proudest moments. (It is sadly ironic, however, that the events that unfolded outside this building nine years later were to bring him such heartache.) A lifelong member of ICCS, Tao gave a myriad of talks on subjects ranging from Confucius to modern-day Chinese science. Also serving as president of the society for many terms, he helped to produce the quarterly newsletter. It is a tribute to his dedication to the ICCS that Tao delivered a lecture entitled 'Emergent China' to the society literally the day before he died.

As this history illustrates, in addition to his Western scientific interests, Tao had a strong scholarly interest in Chinese history and civilization, especially its contributions to mathematics and astronomy. This is well illustrated in his excellent account of how the fifth-century BCE Chinese scholar Tsu Ch'ung-Chih (Zu Chongji in the modern Pinyin system) found the volume of a sphere using arguments completely different to those of Archimedes and the Greek mathematicians. First apparently given as a lunchtime talk in University College London in 1964, it was published in the *Mathematical Gazette* in 1972: a beautiful example of Tao's clear exposition and grasp of both ancient and modern traditions. That it was subsequently reprinted by the Mathematical Association of America in a book celebrating the history of geometry is a testimony to its quality.

Certainly it was this ability to immerse himself in classical Chinese literature as well as familiarity with modern astronomy that produced what was arguably Tao's greatest scientific work: his analysis of the orbit of Halley's Comet. In a series of outstanding papers, Tao combined his knowledge of Western celestial mechanics with a series of observations of Halley's Comet that he was able to identify in the classical Chinese records, thus refining Western understanding of the comet's orbit and its evolution over time. Tao not only discovered new and accurate historical records of the comet in the Chinese sources, but his work also led to an improved understanding of the non-gravitational forces acting on the comet – demolishing suggestions that a new planet beyond Pluto might be responsible for disturbing the orbit.

Tao's spiritual connection to China, his ability to read both classical and modern Chinese astronomical literature, as well as his excellent grasp of the English language and sense of literary style found their perfect expression when he became founding editor of a noted scientific journal published by Pergamon press. This periodical published translations of significant papers by Chinese astronomers, thus becoming the main means by which astronomers in what was then called 'the West' could access the work of their colleagues in Communist China. Starting as *Chinese Astronomy* in 1977, it simply translated the main articles from *Acta Astronomica Sinica* (itself founded in 1953). But after four volumes and the emergence from issue five (1981) of a new Chinese Journal, *Acta Astrophysica Sinica*, it was renamed *Chinese Astronomy and Astrophysics* – with Tao Kiang as the chief translation editor.

For many years this journal was one of the main means by which Western astronomers kept in touch with the work of their Chinese colleagues. Nowadays, of course, there is no need for such translation journals; but one must remember that when the journal was established the Fall of Saigon had ended the Vietnam War only two years earlier, Mao had been dead for less than one year, and the chaos of his Cultural Revolution was still a potent force. Moreover, it was far from clear how China would develop in the post-Mao era within a heavily polarized Cold War world. As an example of how different that world was, one of the early issues carried an article with the extraordinary and intriguing title 'The Red Sun Will Never Set on Purple Mountain Observatory' – arguing for the central role of Marxist dialectic in astronomy.

Tao's other great service to enhancing connections between Chinese astronomy and that of the West was to facilitate the readmission of China to the International Astronomical Union (IAU). The IAU was established in 1919 as a founding scientific union in the International Research Council (subsequently renamed as ICSU, the International Council of Scientific Unions and now simply the International Council for Science). The People's Republic of China had resigned from the IAU in 1959 in protest at the recognition of Taiwan – and was insisting that it would only accept readmission if the IAU withdrew recognition from Taiwan. As chance would have it, Patrick Wayman had been elected as Assistant Secretary General of the IAU in 1976; thus when the executive committee of the IAU met in Dublin in 1978, the 'China question' was put on the agenda. As the official minutes of the meeting record, under item 23:

> The discussion of the People's Republic of China, adjourned earlier, was reopened after a brief informal meeting with Professor Tao Kiang who had reported on his impressions during his visit in China. It was felt that visits of the members of the executive committee would be welcome in China. Professor Wayman said that he expects to be invited to China and that he would go there as Director of the Dunsink Observatory. The President considered the possibility of his going to China early in 1979 and felt that an immediately

following visit to Taiwan would be useful. A suggestion was made that China should be invited to send observers to the Montreal General Assembly.

In his history of Dunsink, Professor Wayman records that he did in fact visit China in April/May 1979 'ostensibly to give lectures and make personal contacts with Chinese astronomers' – but in reality to discuss with officials of the Ministry for Foreign Affairs a form of words under which Chinese membership might be fully restored. Eventually, at the Montreal General Assembly, agreement was reached that there was only one China (this was a key point for both Taiwan and the mainland), but that it could be represented by two adhering bodies, one from Taipei and one from Beijing. As a result, the whole of China, both mainland and Taiwan, was finally readmitted to the ICSU at the Patras General Assembly in 1982.

Reading between the lines, it seems clear that it was Tao Kiang who laid the ground work for this normalization of relations between China and the international scientific community. Certainly it is hard to believe that Patrick Wayman's diplomacy would have been so effective had he not had the benefit of Tao's wise counsel and deep understanding of Chinese culture.

This understanding extended to Tao's private life as well. Although not formally belonging to any religion, Tao was a spiritual being, taking great joy in studying a wide range of both Eastern and Western philosophies including theosophy, Buddhism, Christianity and atheism. However, it was his favourite maxim, stemming from Confucius, 'what you do not like, do not do to others' that brought him to become a Humanist in his last years. A lively debater with broad interests, Tao was also active in the Probus Discussion Group, in which he keenly anticipated being informed about and querying the world at large.

A lighter side to Tao was his great love of wine. Although careful not to over-imbibe, the advent of the vacuum extractor pump meant that there were always several bottles, including his favourite Auslese Riesling, on the go for anybody interested. He was one of the first members of Dublin's Preamble Wine Club, having met the gobsmacked founder of the club following his rendition of 'Danny Boy' in the amphitheatre at Knossus!

After retirement in the mid-90s, Tao and Trudi moved to Bray, County Wicklow, to be nearer their children and grandchildren and to allow Tao to enjoy hillwalking without the long commute. At last having time to indulge his love of music, Tao took up singing as a tenor with the Bray Choral Society, practising daily while accompanying himself on his beloved piano. His mid-life annoyance at his 'disrespectful, disobedient' children had much earlier given way to deep pride as they followed their own paths in life: Rosalind as a software designer, Ingmar as a musician, Sophie as a geneticist, Tanya as a curator of photography and Jessica as a film critic. He spent many happy hours with his adoring grandchildren Ben, Heidi, Oisin, Eve, Lara and Seamus Tao – with whom he again could be a child, looking at the wonders of the universe as if for the first time.

For such a rich life, in which his consuming interest in astronomy extended to building cultural bridges between a young Republic of Ireland and an emerging People's Republic of China, a fitting and final tribute to Tao remains literally in the heavens. On 10 July 1983 Edward Boswell, a former student of Tao Kiang's at University College London, working at Anderson Mesa station of the Lowell Observatory in Arizona, discovered Minor Planet number 3751. By longstanding tradition, the discoverer of a minor planet (or asteroid) is allowed to propose a name for the object. Thus it is that Minor Planet 3751 is now officially named Kiang in honour of his mentor, Tao Kiang, who brought so many riches to Irish, as well as to international, astronomy.

References

Kiang, T. (1955), 'Colour Excesses of B Stars and the Inner Spiral Arm', *Annales d'Astrophysique*, vol. 18, pp. 76–7.

Kiang, T. (1966), 'Random Fragmentation in Two and Three Dimensions', *Zeitschrift fuer Astrophysik*, no. 64, pp. 433–9.

Kiang, T. (1972), 'An Old Chinese Way of Finding the Volume of a Sphere', *The Mathematical Gazette*, vol. 56, pp. 88–91.

Kiang, T. (1972), 'The Past Orbit of Halley's Comet', *Memoirs of the Royal Astronomical Society*, no. 76, pp. 27–66.

Kiang, T. (1973), 'The Cause of the Residuals in the Motion of Halley's Comet', *Monthly Notices of the Royal Astronomical Society*, vol. 162, pp. 271–87.

Pritchard, C., ed. (2003), *The Changing Shape of Geometry – Celebrating a Century of Geometry and Geometry Teaching*, Cambridge University Press.

Wayman, P. A. (1987), 'Dunsink Observatory, 1785–1985: A Bicentennial History', *Historical Studies in Irish Science and Technology*, no. 7, Dublin: Royal Dublin Society.

Who Are We? Chinese Migrants in the Republic of Ireland

Lu Zhouxiang and Wu Weiyi

Despite being a small and relatively peripheral country – with a population of only 4.5 million and a territory of about seventy thousand square kilometres – the Republic of Ireland has become an increasingly globalized nation since the late 1990s. How has this happened? The influx of foreign migrants (that is, foreign nationals who study, work, or live in Ireland) from around the world has irreversibly changed the face of this Celtic nation. Its rapid economic development in the 1990s and early 2000s – known as the 'Celtic Tiger' era – brought prosperity to Ireland, transforming it into a popular immigration destination in the second half of the 1990s. This sudden influx contrasts sharply with the massive outflow in the nineteenth and early twentieth centuries of Irish migrants to the United States, the United Kingdom (UK), Canada and Australia.

Among those foreign migrants who travelled to Ireland to chase their dreams are the Chinese. In the six decades since the first group of Chinese migrants arrived in Ireland, the Chinese in Ireland have changed from being a largely 'unseen' small group to becoming the fifth largest population of non-European Economic Area nationals in the country. How have their new lives evolved? What challenges does this new way of life pose for their sense of identity? And how have they managed to integrate into Irish society?

For all migrant groups to a new culture, their new identity – which in many ways depends on how they are in turn identified – is often interpreted as being simply 'Chinese': that is, as one homogeneous ethnic group. This is a radical simplification of their actual situation, as it does not take into account the many historical and structural differentiations within the group itself. In fact, only when the diversity of Chinese migrants is recognized can their different states of integration – and their attitudes towards related issues – be actually revealed.

To try to respond to these issues, eleven interviews were conducted to obtain first-hand, in-depth accounts. The interviewees include a businessman, a university lecturer, a self-employed worker, two white-collar workers, a chef, a restaurant manager, a sports-club coach and three students, ranging in ages from 18 to 60. They were living in Dublin, Cork, Kerry, Kildare, Limerick and Galway. Five were female; six were male. Interviews with them varied in duration from forty-five to sixty minutes. Evaluating their responses involved, to some degree, acknowledging factors such as when and from where they migrated, which in turn have resulted in their quite disparate perceptions of such issues as integration and identity.

A Brief History of Chinese Migrants in Ireland
The first wave of migration (1950s–1990s)

The first group of Chinese migrants in Ireland came largely from Hong Kong. Due to the colonial relationship between Hong Kong and the United Kingdom, the UK has historically been a popular destination for Hong Kong migrants. From the 1950s on, Hong Kong migrants living in the UK began to settle in the Republic of Ireland, with the following decades seeing a slow but steady increase in its Chinese population. Most of these migrants were ethnic Chinese from Hong Kong or from Malaysia and other South-East Asian countries.

The majority of these early Chinese migrants worked in the catering industry, predominantly in the Chinese restaurants and takeaways that started to appear in Ireland in the late 1950s and 1960s. In fact, many of them migrated to Ireland from the UK because of the saturation of the UK Chinese restaurant/takeaway market. Take Cathay, one of the first Chinese restaurants in Dublin, as an example: the restaurant was opened in Kildare Street in September 1957 by a Chinese Malay businessman from London. He had travelled to Ireland on holiday and saw a business opportunity in Dublin. He then moved to Dublin with his family and recruited a chef and two assistants from Hong Kong to get the restaurant up and running.[1]

Many of these early Chinese migrants came to Ireland alone in their teens or early twenties to join relatives or friends in the Chinese restaurant business. It was common practice for these young migrants eventually to open their own restaurants and takeaways in Ireland using their newfound skills and experience. This, in turn, provided more jobs for new migrants from Hong Kong, Malaysia, Indonesia and other South-East Asian countries, resulting in the further expansion of the Chinese restaurant and takeaway sector in Ireland in the following decades. Interviewee A and her husband were among those early Chinese migrants who moved to Ireland and joined the catering industry. She recalled:

> My sister immigrated to Ireland from Vietnam in the 1980s. After settling down, she invited me and my husband to Ireland. Later, my four other sisters and brothers also joined us. Back in the 1980s, you could barely see any Chinese people in Ireland. The Irish people were very friendly to us. We received a lot of support and help from the locals. We studied English in a language school for several years and later my husband opened a Chinese takeaway shop in Dublin.

Another group of early Chinese migrants to Ireland was made up of young professionals with college degrees. Some were first-generation migrants from Hong Kong, Malaysia and other South-East Asian countries; others were second-generation Chinese migrants from the UK. They arrived in Ireland later, in the 1980s and 1990s. Because of their educational backgrounds (compared to the former group) they normally took up better-paid jobs in both the public and private sectors, thus obtaining higher socio-economic status in Irish society.

The second wave of migration (early 2000s–today)

The rapid economic growth in Ireland in the 1990s led to a second wave of Chinese migration in the early 2000s, when large numbers of Mainland Chinese professionals and students came to the country. Due to the labour shortages experienced during the Celtic Tiger era, Irish business organizations had called for and achieved reform of the old visa system, which had a long history of restrictions on immigration. Consequently, an increasing number of work permits began to be issued to non-EU migrants. In 1993, the government issued 1,103 work permits. By 2001, the figure had risen to more than 36,000.[2]

The Chinese were among those non-EU nationals who embraced Ireland in the Celtic Tiger era. From the late 1990s, the number of a new generation of Chinese immigrants – consisting of Mandarin-speaking professionals from Mainland China – began to rise. At the same time, with the upsurge of the Chinese economy, an increasing number of upper-middle-class families began sending their children to Ireland to study. This was facilitated by the Irish government's 'Asia strategy', which encouraged the Irish higher-education sector to recruit students from China. According to a 2012 survey by an Irish consulting agency, the majority of Chinese migrants in Ireland were student-visa holders.[3] Of all foreign national groups in Ireland, the number of Chinese students was the highest.[4]

Because of the steady influx of young professionals and students from Mainland China, according to the Irish Census of 2011, the number of Chinese migrants in Ireland has continued to grow over the last two decades. Significantly, the Chinese community here was soon dominated by young migrants. By 2006, a total of more than eleven thousand Chinese people were living in Ireland – an increase of 91 per cent on the 2002 figure of under six thousand (Census, 2011). Yet, before the influx of Mainland Chinese immigrants, the Chinese used to be a quite small group in Ireland.

On the Diversity of Chinese Migrants

Citizenship status: initial classification

As the above review shows, in the course of two distinct waves of migration, Chinese migrants in Ireland have become a quite diversified group. A most obvious disparity is their citizenship status, which is due largely to their different migration times and origins. For example, the Chinese British who came to Ireland between the 1950s and 1990s were not affected by their citizenship status, unlike the subsequent migrants from Mainland China. Why is this important? Because it is associated with migrants' access to social supports, facilities and other benefits; thus, taken with the stereotyped and negative perceptions of migrants in the host society, citizenship status has become 'a key factor in integration in Ireland'.[5] All migrants to Ireland face considerable economic and institutional obstacles.

But adopting Irish citizenship can be a particularly hard decision for migrants from Mainland China because dual citizenship is not acknowledged by the Chinese government. Interviewee C's narration explains the trade-off that many other migrants may also have had to make and the complex psychology behind it:

> After more than ten years of hard work, I finally opened a small Chinese takeaway shop. My wife and son joined me in 2014. Although I lost my Chinese citizenship, I am still Chinese. This fact won't change. My son and wife will keep their Chinese citizenship because this is the best solution for our family. We can travel between and live in the two countries without barriers. The Irish passport offers me a sense of security and stability. There is no need to go to the immigration office to renew my visa anymore and now I can finally bid farewell to all those restrictions on foreign nationals. My family and I are also entitled to all the social protections offered by the State, which makes me feel more secure.

Education and occupation: further differentiations

Citizenship status is an instant form of categorization, whereas education and occupation have cumulative effects on individuals' socio-economic status – thereby further differentiating them into various social strata.

As the migration history summarized above shows, catering has been a conventional business for Chinese migrants in Ireland. When the early Chinese migrants secured footholds in Ireland, they started to bring over relatives to support and expand their restaurants and takeaways. As a useful means of mutual support, this practice has been carried on by subsequent migrants from Mainland China. Nowadays, chefs and cooks (19 per cent), sales assistants (9 per cent) and waiters and waitresses (9 per cent) are the three main jobs held by Chinese migrants. According to *Business in China*'s 2012 survey, fewer than 11 per cent of Chinese migrants own property in Ireland, while 60 per cent of the interviewees were living in shared houses or apartments. This survey reveals the lower social position of Chinese migrants taken as a whole, as well as an obvious pyramid structure to this group.

The context for these statistics tends to be complex and sometimes intertwined. Historically, Chinese migrants have consisted of a large proportion of simple labourers with limited education and skills. This disadvantage, combined with the various barriers faced by immigrant workers, has led to a common perception of Chinese migrants as inferior. Now, after two decades of a continuous influx of students, the demographic structure of Chinese migrants has changed, particularly in terms of educational attainment. Theoretically, young, competent students should enhance the social mobility of the group and increase dynamism within the group. However, as suggested by the data, this has not been realized. Perhaps this is because Chinese students, in terms of numbers, constitute only the middle stratum of the pyramid structure. In actuality, this is a socio-structurally fluid stratum. As non–EU nationals, these students face many obstacles in terms of employment and residence. In response to all these difficulties and restrictions, some students may leave for other Western countries to pursue better career-development opportunities. Many others choose to return and use their new degrees and skills for self-development in China, where they can benefit from a lower cost of living and family support, as well as fulfilling family obligations – an important consideration for all Chinese persons.

One difficulty is that only a very small number of Chinese graduates can find full-time jobs by obtaining the employment permits to work in Ireland demanded for all non-EEA nationals. In general, applicants for employment permits must have a minimum annual remuneration (pay) of €30,000. All new applicants must provide evidence that a labour market needs test has been carried out. This test requires that the vacancy must have been advertised with the Department of Social Protection (DSP) employment services/EURES (European Employment Services) network for two weeks, in a national newspaper for at least three days and in either a local newspaper or on a jobs website for three days. This is to ensure that an EEA or Swiss national cannot be found to fill the vacancy.

Another obstacle forcing the majority of Chinese graduates to leave the country lies in Ireland's immigration rules. According to these, student-visa holders are not entitled to apply for long-term residency, regardless of how many years they have spent in Ireland. In order to remain in the country, non-EU students must be enrolled in academic programmes and renew their student visas annually.

After the 2008 financial crisis, many Chinese student-visa holders left the country because their income from part-time jobs could no longer cover their tuition fees. On top of these are the increased fees for registration with the Garda National Immigration Bureau (GNIB) for legally resident non-EEA nationals who have entered Ireland with the intention of residing in Ireland for a period of more than three months. While these must register on a regular basis with their local immigration registration officer to gain a certificate of registration (GNIB Registration Card, replaced by the new Irish Residence Permit from 11 December 2017), fees have risen from €100 to €150 in 2008 and to €300 in 2012. To counter these difficulties, in 2012 the Irish government introduced the Student Probationary Extension, which allowed non-EEA national students who had first registered their residence in Ireland as students on or before 31 December 2004 and who commenced their studies in Ireland on or before then to register for a two-year probationary period. At the conclusion of the two-year probationary period, eligible students would be entitled to apply for long-term residency in the state. This policy was warmly welcomed by those Chinese students who wished to stay in the country.

Yet, despite such measures, the number of Chinese residents in Ireland has declined over the last few years. By 2016, a total of 9,575 Chinese nationals were living in Ireland – a decrease of 12 per cent on the 2011 figure (Census, 2016).

Origin and generation of identity: self-categorization

Interestingly, while being categorized and further differentiated by historical and structural forces, migrants also carry out a self-categorization process based on a range of standards. For Chinese migrants in Ireland, an important criterion is origin before migration.

Chinese migrants from the UK or Asian countries and those from Mainland China see themselves as two distinct groups. The factors that matter in making this distinction are, among others: citizenship status, background and experience, lifestyles, language preferences and competence, ideals and values. Migrants from Mainland China also divide themselves into separate groups, of which migrants from Fujian province and those from the north-eastern provinces are among the most prominent. For them, local dialect difference is a main cultural factor that hinders communication and further interaction. Moreover, cultural indicators that are easily perceivable in daily life and historical and socio-economic backgrounds have a profound influence in activating individuals' group awareness and relevant behaviour patterns. To be more specific, the tradition of emigration in Fujian province dates back to the nineteenth century, with the primary destination being South-East Asia and North America. The massive outflow of migrants from the north-eastern provinces did not occur, however, until the 1990s, when large numbers of workers were made redundant from state-owned enterprises.

The interviewees' descriptions reflect those inherent differences. Interviewee C's experience demonstrates the continuity of the emigration tradition in Fujian:

> In my home town in Fuqing County, Fujian Province, migration to developed countries is a popular practice among young people. Japan, Australia, Canada and the United States are top destinations. Back in the 1980s, many of the young people would smuggle their way into those countries and work in Chinese restaurants. Young fellows who choose to stay in Fuqing face a lot of pressure because other people working in Western countries always send money back home and they build big fancy houses in the village … old people will say things like 'decent fellows go abroad while lazy people stay at home'.

After generations of this practice, working abroad has become accepted as a convention in Fujian. However, people in other parts of China tend to evaluate the specific costs and benefits of migration, thus being inclined to move to countries with higher economic benefits.

In such calculations, gains are balanced against possible losses in China to justify the risks undertaken in the first place. As Interviewee Z, who works in a hotel in Cork city, recalled:

> I am not good at studying. So, after graduating from secondary school, I joined a vocational school in Shenyang city and studied hotel management. I then moved to Ireland in 2003 and began to work as a waiter in a hotel in Cork. I really enjoy my work and life here in Ireland. Although I am not rich, I am happy with my income. In this country, there is no intense competition and there is no big gap between the rich and the poor. In China, the monthly salary for a hotel waiter is only around €300. You can barely feed yourself with that type of salary. I feel that I am very lucky compared to my friends in China, who are still struggling in the job market.

Interviewee L, a computer scientist from northern China, commented:

> I had a good job in Beijing but I was separated from my family because my wife was working in another city in eastern China. After we migrated to Ireland, although my wife can't work because of the immigration rules, my salary is good enough to support the whole family. Ireland is free from air pollution. There is no food safety issue. You wouldn't be able to 'buy' this good environment in Beijing, even if you were a multi-millionaire. My daughter is now enjoying Ireland's world-class education and social welfare systems. She no longer needs to face the intense competition and pressure in Chinese society. We also plan to have a second child. If we had stayed in China [and had a second child], I would lose my job and face a big fine due to the 'one child policy'. By migrating to Ireland, we are free in our family planning now.[6]

Thus their historical and socio-economic backgrounds influence not only migrants' perceptions and attitudes but also their avoidance of actual risks. For migrants from Fujian and other places with a similar tradition, their social networks are usually formed through kinship and long-term friendship. In this way, they can be assured of peer support when faced with difficulties and grow human capital within their networks. In the same way, Chinese migrants also tend to form their social circles with Chinese colleagues or neighbours. Such temporary networks are usually fragile due to the instability of migrants' jobs, residence and so on. In such relatively loose and fragile networks, an individual immigrant often struggles alone and thus is more exposed to the dangers of poverty and marginalization.

In the above discussion, students from Mainland China are excluded because their origins are scattered all over the country. More importantly, the student community is essentially different from the working population with regard to social classification and self-categorization. Because their environments and activities are relatively identical, differentiation among students is not as evident as that between the subgroups mentioned earlier. Another community that also has a special self-perception is that made up of the descendants of Chinese migrants who have grown up in Ireland with the hyphenated identity Chinese-Irish. With that ambiguous and sometimes ambivalent dual identity, there is little wonder that they tend to categorize themselves as distinct from other Chinese migrants and also from the rest of society.[7]

Implications of Diversity for Interaction and Identity

As the examples above illustrate, despite their common nationality, Chinese migrants are both socially stratified and culturally differentiated. Therefore, it is vital for Irish society – and especially for its policymakers – to understand the historical, socio-economic and cognitive contexts of their diversity, as well as its implications for the integration and identity of individual migrants.

Heterogeneous Chinese identity

The question of migrants' integration and identity are usually discussed in the context of ethnic relations. A main focus of that discussion are the ethnic boundaries, which, according to scholars such as Benedict Anderson, are both real and imagined, instrumental and symbolic, ambiguous and dynamic – and hence always subject to negotiation and construction.[8] However, most empirical studies on Chinese migrants in foreign countries define that boundary in terms of a homogeneous Chinese identity – and therefore not from the perspective that emphasizes process and transformation but one that tends to be essentialist and static. But as the above analysis of in-group diversity demonstrates, any notion of an abstract Chinese identity is actually understood and performed quite heterogeneously by migrants from the various subgroups.

In the 2011 census, nearly eighteen thousand respondents ticked the option of 'Chinese ethnic or cultural background', while almost eleven thousand declared themselves Chinese nationals. Apparently, for those from Taiwan, Hong Kong and Macau, as well as Malaysia, Singapore and other countries and regions, Chinese identity is not defined by nationality or ethnicity alone but more often by inherited and acquired cultural characteristics such as language, diet, customs and beliefs. Consequently, group boundaries and intergroup relations are often interpreted and addressed by these particular migrants within a cultural context, whereas Chinese nationals in Ireland often have a stronger political sensitivity. In other words, the cultural, affective and socio-political significances of Chinese identity matter differently to migrants from different backgrounds. Nevertheless, symbolic and instrumental connotations may also be interconnected in particular circumstances. For instance, Interviewee B, a Chinese British national who was born in Hong Kong, expressed a sense of pride while talking about the rise of China:

> Back in the 1960s and 1970s, when China was still very poor, overseas Chinese occasionally suffered racism and discrimination. Now China has become a major player in world economy. I can feel a change in Western people's attitudes toward China and Chinese people, and this makes me feel proud.

Sometimes, however, the descendants of migrants from Hong Kong and other South-East Asian countries 'opt out' of their Chinese identity for political and ideological reasons. This has become more evident since the 'Occupy Central' movement, a civil-disobedience campaign, was initiated by Hong Kong political activists in 2015. As Interviewee G, a young Hong Kong-born professional in Dublin, stated:

> To be honest, I don't like people to call me Chinese. Hong Kong is totally different from China. I am a Hong Konger. After Hong Kong was handed over to China by Britain, Hong Kong people's lives were badly affected by Chinese influence. Many Chinese tourists don't respect Hong Kong's culture and law. They rush into Hong Kong to buy baby formula and empty the shelves in shopping malls. Local shops and restaurants were forced to close down to give way to luxury retail chain stores. Pregnant Chinese women came to Hong Kong in large numbers to give birth so that their babies would get Hong Kong citizenship. This resulted in the shortage of maternity beds in hospitals. Chinese investors also pushed up property prices in Hong Kong, making ordinary people's lives very difficult. Now China wants to tighten its control over Hong Kong by interfering in its electoral reform. Hong Kong people are losing their freedom.

Certainly the constructed nature of ethnic boundaries indicates that future scholars ought to pay more attention to the fashioning processes underlying Chinese identity, as well as the contextual salience of its multiple meanings.

Stratified integration

Chinese migrants of different socio-economic statuses tend to be stratified in terms of their competences and degrees of integration. A critical factor in stratified integration is language ability, which is quoted by most interviewees as a key barrier to integration. As Interviewee H, who migrated to Ireland in the 1980s, commented:

> Because of the language barrier, it is difficult for us to understand and integrate into Irish society. We live in a small circle surrounded by Chinese friends and relatives. We don't know what is happening in Irish society. Although we have more Irish friends now, but we still feel that we are isolated from Irish society. After all these years, the language barrier is still there. My English is only OK for daily communication, but not for in-depth communication. For example,

> I could only understand a small part of the school principal's speeches at my daughter's graduation ceremony. I wanted to join other parents to chat but I can't understand them well.

Interviewees also pointed out other barriers, such as knowledge of Irish history and culture, which tend to affect the scope and depth of their contact with local people. As Interviewee H recounted:

> For me, there is no language barrier when I chat with my Irish friends ... When they begin to talk about Irish stuff, for example the GAA, it becomes very difficult to catch up because I only have a limited knowledge of Irish history, culture and society. I remember one time they talked about Freemasonry for the whole night. Although I could understand the language, I couldn't understand the content. It was like if an Irish person sits by a group of Chinese people who are talking about the last emperor of the Tang Dynasty.

Because socio-economic status is normally positively correlated with the other listed elements, high-skilled Chinese professionals are presumably more integrated than low-skilled, working-class Chinese migrants, who tend to live in a small and isolated 'Chinese circle'. Most of these low-skilled workers are in the catering industry. They work long hours and rarely have time for entertainment and leisure activities. The majority of them are striving to save money. Some send their savings back to China to support their family members. This is the primary concern of Interviewee S, a chef in a Chinese restaurant in Dublin:

> I used to work as a chef in my home town. The salary in Ireland is much higher than that in China so I moved to Ireland in 2006. By doing so, I can save more money and invest it in my children's education. My two children are in college now. They need money to cover their tuition fees and living expenses. Life in Ireland is not easy. I share a room with my colleagues. My social circle is very small. My friends are Chinese colleagues from the restaurant. After all these years I still can't speak English. I am 'deaf' and 'blind' and I don't know what is happening in Irish society. My plan is to work in

Ireland for another few years and then go back to China to reunite with my family. As we Chinese people always say: 'The bitter must come before the sweet, and that also makes the sweet all the sweeter.'

Unlike working-class Chinese migrants, who often stick to small but close social circles, highly skilled Chinese professionals face fewer language, social and economic barriers. They are more actively willing to integrate into Irish society. However, they may also experience more integration pressure and identity anxiety. The previously mentioned Interviewee B described a strong consciousness of his Hong Kong/Chinese identity and explained the reason behind it:

> Our family moved to the UK when I was still a kid. I am in the so-called second generation of overseas Chinese. I grew up in the UK and I am a native English speaker. I moved to Ireland in the 1980s and established my family here. But when I walk on the street, will people think that I am British or Irish? Of course not. Why? Because I don't look like a Westerner. For me, the passport is only a legal document. It has nothing to do with my ethnic/national identity ... I am a Hong Konger, and I am Chinese. This is a fact and I also educate my children about this fact. They are the third generation of overseas Chinese. I don't want them to get confused about their identity.

Interviewee E, a college graduate from Inner Mongolia, arrived in Ireland in 2002 and studied at a private English school for two years. After that, he found a job in a local sports club thanks to his college degree, and then established a family in Ireland. Compared to Interviewee B, his attitude is more ambivalent:

> My family is here and Ireland is my second home country. My wife is Irish and my two children are also Irish. I sometimes thought about getting Irish citizenship, but I've decided to keep my Chinese citizenship ... In terms of integration, language is no longer a barrier for me, but Chinese culture is so different from Irish culture – the ways of thinking and communicating are so different. Yes, you can integrate into Irish society to some extent, but full integration is a mission impossible.

The perceptions of Interviewee B and Interviewee E suggest that, as more capable and autonomous migrants, Chinese professionals may actively integrate into Irish society for instrumental concerns but still feel distanced from Irish culture and mainstream values for symbolic and emotional reasons.

Hyphenated identity vs. short-term residents

Second-generation, foreign-born Chinese are quite different from students coming from Mainland China. These are two special subgroups with respect to their circumstances and perceptions of integration and identification. As pointed out by Nicola Yau, 'the second generation are not migrants but rather the product of migration'.[9] As a minority within a minority group, they are quite conscious about their in-between situation, their hyphenated identity. Based on empirical evidence gathered through interviews and an online forum, Yau argues that second-generation Chinese are often forced to identify as Chinese due to the restrictive nature of 'Irishness' (being white) and the pressures of both marginalization and racialization. In other words, they are not regarded as fully or properly Irish either by themselves or by society.[10]

In this context, hyphenated identity (Chinese-Irish or Irish-born Chinese), even though racialized, is useful in providing them with some sense of belonging. Interviewee F, who immigrated into Ireland in the 1980s with her husband, spoke of the difficulties and confusion experienced by her children, which indicates that adopting a hyphenated identity was a strategy they acquired or an answer they eventually figured out during the self-identification process:

> I have three children. They were born in Ireland in the 1980s. When they were young, they felt that they were Irish. But when they came across strangers on the street, people would say that they were Chinese. They got confused about their identity from time to time. They couldn't understand why people wouldn't acknowledge them as 'Irish'. But now they are no longer confused about their Chinese identity. They explain to people that they are Irish-born Chinese.

Chinese students, however, are unlikely to have identity confusion because they are socially regarded – and self-identify – as Chinese in every sense: in terms of nationality, ethnicity, language and culture. Thus they show a much lower motivation to integrate in comparison with both second-generation Chinese and Erasmus students from European countries. These young people tend to spend their spare time with Chinese classmates and friends, generally preferring 'Chinese-style' leisure activities like going out for dinner rather than more Irish activities such as going out to pubs and clubs. As Interviewee G stated:

> I used to live in the university's student apartment and I shared with several Irish and American students. They liked to go to pubs in the evening. I know pub culture is very important in Ireland, but I don't like to drink. Most of my Chinese friends, especially the girls, don't like to drink either. However, it was difficult for me to say 'no' if they invited me. So, a few months later, I moved out and began to share a house with a couple of Chinese students from the university. We organized a dinner party every week. Everyone would contribute one dish. By doing so, we could enjoy a variety of traditional food from different parts of China. We chatted during the dinner and shared our experiences studying and living in Ireland. It was great fun.

Financial resources are believed to be another barrier to social integration for Chinese students. As Interviewee I explained:

> I do have Irish friends but it is too expensive to integrate into Irish society. Irish socializing is pub-oriented. In the past, my Irish friends always liked to invite me to go out for a pint, but normally I would refuse – only because I can't afford it. A pint in the pub costs five euro. I only have thirty euro for my weekly living expenses! How can I afford those expensive pub rounds? I can't just join them but contribute nothing. So after I refused [their invitation] several times, they no longer invite me. Some of my Irish friends believe that I am a nerd. I felt embarrassed but I don't know how to explain this to them.

Exclusive 'Chinese circles' and introverted dispositions appear to be common representations of Chinese students. From their own perspectives, however, active integration is neither practicable nor desirable considering their temporary residence, high mobility and dissociated position in Irish society. According to a recently conducted survey by Cao Yu, the majority of Chinese students have no intention of staying after graduation due to various concerns and restrictions, such as the immigration policy, job opportunities and family obligations in China. Some Chinese students see Ireland as a stepping stone for migration to other English-speaking countries like Australia, the United States and Canada, which have bigger Chinese populations, more jobs and relatively welcoming immigration policies. As Interviewee G, a postgraduate student at University College Cork, states:

> After graduating from Shanghai University, I decided to come to Ireland to study international business. My parents supported me. In Shanghai, it is popular for middle-class families to send their children abroad to study. Ireland is a beautiful country and the standard of living is quite high. However, Ireland is too small and it is not a country for immigrants. After graduation, I will need a work permit to remain in Ireland, which seems impossible. I am now in the process of applying for a PhD programme offered by a Canadian university. Canada always welcomes young immigrants and Canada has a big Chinese population. My long-term plan is to get my PhD degree, find a job, settle down and eventually bring my parents over to Canada.

To compare the two communities briefly, it appears that some of the second-generation Chinese are plagued by self-doubt and the fear of marginalization and, accordingly, resort to a hyphenated identity to give a sense of stability and togetherness. Conversely, Chinese students, as short-term residents who seem to be more autonomous in remaining dissociated, essentially stay on the fringes of the social system. This suggests that hyphenated identity and cautious dissociation are both strategies configured and consolidated during the negotiation and construction of group boundaries within the Irish community.

Conclusion

In just over half a century, the Chinese in Ireland have changed from being a largely 'unseen' small group to becoming the fifth largest population of non-EEA nationals in the country. In the meantime, Irish society, which used to be relatively homogeneous, both ethnically and culturally, has embraced a wide range of ethnic groups and heterogeneous cultures. These intertwined transformations have created challenges for both groups – Chinese migrants and local Irish people – and also raised fundamental questions for both researchers and policymakers.

As a research area, the subject of Chinese migrants in Ireland – such as their in-group diversity and its implications – is still novel. This essay seeks to draw more attention to this particular group, especially with regard to the need for exploration into encounters between subgroups and long-term studies into their lives. Such a life-course approach would provide researchers with a perspective on human development that ought to be a core value of (im)migration studies. Working from such a perspective, future researchers could track the general social mobility of Chinese migrants across generations, as well as examining integration and identity changes in certain focus groups.

As a country that is 'new to the migration experience', Ireland has been working on an integration strategy that could ensure positive outcomes and enhance social cohesiveness. One such enterprise has been the publication in 2008 of the findings of the UCD Migration and Citizenship Research Initiative through the Immigrant Council of Ireland (see below). Another took place when, in July 2007, the Irish government appointed a Minister for Integration to develop strategies on integration and immigration; that year, €9 million was allocated to the Office for Integration. That office published its first report under the title of 'Migration Nation – Statement on Integration Strategy and Diversity Management' also in 2008. It indicated that the government intended to produce a comprehensive strategy for all legally resident immigrants along with coordinating mechanisms to implement it. Another range of strategies was also expected to be pursued as part of the National Action Plan against Racism.

However, eight years after the establishment of the office, there has been a lack of progress in the field of integration, due largely to the impact of the 2008 financial crisis. That year, the National Consultative Committee on Racism and Interculturalism was closed down because of budget cutbacks. Then, in 2011, after the Office for Integration was also abolished, the country's integration policy was put on hold. Since the Irish economy has begun to recover since 2015, it is to be expected that the government will initiate a new integration strategy in the near future (according to the Office for the Promotion of Migrant Integration). But first – both ideally and practically – the government's new integration policies and strategies must be based upon a comprehensive appreciation of the diversities of each migrant group. In itself this would represent a fresh understanding of the true nature of Chinese migrants to the Republic of Ireland in the last half century.

Further reading

Chu, Hazel (2017), 'Chinese Experience in Ireland Shows Price of Cultural Integration', *The Irish Times*, 13 February.

Feldman, Alice; Gilmartin, Mary; Loyal, Steven and Migge, Bettina (2008), *Getting on: From Migration to Integration: Chinese, Indian, Lithuanian and Nigerian Migrants*, Dublin: Immigrant Council of Ireland.

Yau, N. (2007), 'Celtic Tiger, Hidden Dragon: Exploring Identity among Second Generation Chinese in Ireland', *Translocations* (The Irish Migration, Race and Social Transformation Review), vol. 2, no. 1, pp. 48–69.

Yu Cao (2018), 'Chinese Migrants in Ireland: Current Situation and Future Trend', *Journal of Overseas Chinese History Studies*, no. 1, pp. 71–8.

Endnotes

1   S. McGrath (2012), 'Dublin's First Chinese Restaurants (1956–mid-1960s)', http://comeheretome.com/2012/07/25/dublins-first-chinese-restaurants-1956-mid-1960s/ (accessed 1 February 2016).

2   S. Loyal (2003), 'Welcome to the Celtic Tiger: Racism, Immigration and the State', in C. Coulter and S. Coleman (eds) *The End of Irish History?*, Manchester: Manchester University Press, pp. 74–94.

3   BusinessinChina.ie (2013), 'The Dragon's Voice: A Survey of Chinese People Living, Working and Studying in Ireland', http://www.businessinchina.ie/index.php/the-dragons-voice-2012-survey-results-has-been-released-by-business-in-china/ (accessed 8 February 2016).

4   Central Statistics Office (2012), Census 2011, 'Profile 6 Migration and Diversity – A Profile of Diversity in Ireland', Central Statistics Office, Dublin.

5   Feldman, Alice; Gilmartin, Mary; Loyal, Steven and Migge, Bettina (2008), *Getting On: from Migration to Integration: Chinese, Indian, Lithuanian and Nigerian Migrants*, Immigrant Council of Ireland, Dublin, p. 22.

6   It is worth noting that during the past decade the one-child policy has been gradually relaxed in some provinces. The policy was finally abolished by the Chinese government in 2015. Urban residents are now allowed to have two children – and the current trend is to encourage them to have even more.

7   N. Yau (2007), 'Celtic Tiger, Hidden Dragon: Exploring Identity among Second Generation Chinese in Ireland', *Translocations (The Irish Migration, Race and Social Transformation Review)*, vol. 2, no. 1, pp. 48–69.

8   B. Anderson (1991), *Imagined Communities: Reflections on the Origin and Spread of Nationalism*, London: Verso; R. Bauman (2004), *A World of Others' Words: Cross-Cultural Perspectives on Intertextuality*, Malden, MA: Blackwell Publishing.

9   Yau (2007), p. 59.

10 Ibid., pp. 48–69.

An Emerging Field: Irish Studies in China

Chen Li

China may seem to many an unlikely place for Irish Studies; yet there today it is a rising academic discipline. Following the history of its rise might indicate why, despite huge disparity in size or their vast distance from each other both culturally and geographically, Irish Studies has become a flourishing enterprise in China. Although acknowledged as a distinctive field only in the past decade, it has grown rapidly through both institutional development and scholarly research.

But long before it emerged as a specific discipline, a vivid interest in Irish history and culture, including the production of both translations and critical studies of literature, attracted Chinese intellectuals. Roughly speaking, two major periods can be identified in China's interest in Irish Studies: the early twentieth century and the more contemporary period after the 1990s. The first existed concurrently with China's urge to find literary expression for and solutions to its own political crises, whereas the second coincides with China's rapid modernization and globalization since its opening-up in 1978.

Early Encounters

During the late nineteenth and early twentieth centuries, both China and Ireland were immersed in political turmoil. While Ireland struggled to achieve independence from centuries of British colonization, China was torn by factional warlords as well as foreign threats, in which Britain was a major factor. The British Empire was among the first foreign powers to threaten the rule of the complacent Qing Dynasty. The First Opium War (or the First Anglo-Chinese War, 1839–42) marked the beginning of what Chinese nationalists later generally termed the 'Century of Humiliation' – the period of intervention and domination by Western powers and Japan in China between 1839 and 1949. Even after the Republic of China was founded in 1912 to replace the Qing Dynasty, the country's central authority still waxed and waned in response to warlordism (1916–28), the Japanese invasion (1931–45) and a long civil war (1927–49).

Despite their similar goals of seeking cultural solutions to political crises, however, Irish and Chinese scholars turned in radically different directions. Led by W. B. Yeats, Irish Revivalists looked to an ancient precolonial Celtic heritage for inspiration, whereas the new generation of Chinese scholars, disillusioned with the oppressive, long-existing dominance of Confucianism, looked to the West for new viewpoints and values. Motivated initially by the practical aim of learning advanced technology from the West in order to resist invasion, these efforts evolved into an embrace of literature and culture as well. The New Culture Movement of the 1910s and 1920s – a 'literary revolution' in its true sense – thus paved the way for a modern period of a Chinese literature remarkably different from its precedents.

Such early studies demonstrate that one may date Irish Studies in China all the way back to the early twentieth century – although clearly not named as such at that time, as 'Ireland' was not yet recognized as an independent nation. Early encounters occurred between Chinese and Irish scholars, especially during China's New Culture Movement. Scholars like Lu Xun (1881–1936), Mao Dun (1896–1981) and Guo Moruo (1892–1978), disillusioned with traditional Chinese culture, advocated a turn to Western culture and values as represented by democracy and science. The Irish independence cause and its associated literary movement (known as the Irish Literary Revival) – which ran almost parallel with China's efforts to seek national independence – provided a valuable inspiration for such scholars in proposing possible political and cultural solutions to China's then pressing problems.

Not surprisingly, during this period consistent efforts were made to introduce Irish politics and literature to the Chinese reader. Journals like *The Eastern Miscellany* (1904–48) and *Fiction Monthly* (1910–) gave special attention to Ireland. A search of the database of *The Eastern Miscellany* with 'Ireland' as the key word reveals more than eight hundred results during the four decades of the journal's existence, with a peak of seventy-two articles reached in 1921. Quite a lot of these focus on the Irish political situation, with titles like 'Irish Home Rule' (by Zhang Xiechen [1912], vol. 9, no. 1), 'The Truth of the Irish Rebellion' (by Xu Jiaqing [1916], vol. 13, no. 8) and 'The Historical Relationship between Ireland and Great Britain, and Their Negotiation Process' (by Yu Shixiu [1922], vol. 19, no. 4).

Literature – in this period closely associated with political change in both Ireland and China – played a dynamic role, the Irish Dramatic Movement in particular drawing keen attention from Chinese scholars. In March 1920, *The Eastern Miscellany* (vol. 17, no. 6) published W. B. Yeats's play *The Hour-Glass* (1903) translated by Mao Dun, together with Mao's important critical essay 'A Counter-Current in Contemporary Literature – New Writings in Ireland'. In that essay, Mao Dun summarized the 'counter-current' feature of the Irish literary movement as follows: 'While people were questioning the future and favouring cosmopolitanism, the Irish were paying particular attention to their own history and national traits. The new Irish literature formed a unique school of its own'.

As is quite understandable, due to their own cultural crisis, Yeats drew Chinese scholars' attention first as an activist for the nationalist cause rather than purely for the sake of his artistic achievements. When Yeats was awarded the Nobel Prize in 1923, his reception reached new heights in China, with many translated works published and a special issue of *Fiction Monthly* dedicated to him ([1923], vol. 14, no. 12). During this period, Wang Tongzhao (1897–1957) and Zheng Zhenduo (1898–1958) became the major translators of Yeats, as well as authoring criticism about his works.

At this critical time for China, other important Irish writers were also translated and introduced to the Chinese public. Besides George Bernard Shaw and Oscar Wilde, who were usually labelled as British writers, Lady Gregory, George Russell (A.E.) and John Millington Synge were certainly placed within an Irish context.

Most of Shaw's and Wilde's plays were translated into Chinese at that time. Lady Gregory's patriotic play *The Rising of the Moon* was translated and adapted to Chinese stages with great success. Mao Dun and Zhao Jingshen (1902–85) both made frequent contributions to *Fiction Monthly*, updating the latest information on the Irish literary landscape. Then, in 1929, Tian Han (1898–1968), a founding father of China's modern drama and the lyric writer of China's national anthem, published *An Introduction to Contemporary Irish Drama* (Shanghai: Southeast Bookstore), making it the most consistent effort so far in China to review major Irish playwrights and their works during the Revival period.

Recent studies provide more detailed and more interesting facts about those early encounters. Ni Ping's *George Bernard Shaw and China* (2001), written in Chinese, offers a well-researched history of Shaw's trip to China in 1933; whereas Kay Li's *Bernard Shaw and China: Cross-Cultural Encounters* (2009), published in English by the University Press of Florida, works from an overseas Chinese's perspective to examine this significant literary encounter. A long serial poem entitled *Victorious in Death* written by Guo Moruo in 1920 was rediscovered by Jerusha McCormack during her research on China–Ireland relationships (an essay on this subject appears in this book on pp. 56–78). Guo wrote this poem upon learning of the hunger strike by the Irish politician Terence MacSwiney (1879–1920). With lines like 'Dear sons of Ireland / The spirit of freedom will ever stand by you', Guo paid tribute to MacSwiney's voluntary death for the cause of national independence.

Nor is such cross-cultural interest limited to politics. For example, Yeats's interest in Chinese philosophies has been explored by recent scholars. In his 1996 essay 'Eastern Elements in Yeats's Poetry', Fu Hao, a leading Yeats translator and researcher in China, inspects how Yeats's flawed knowledge of Indian, Japanese and Chinese philosophies functions in his poetry, a perspective quite helpful to Chinese readers who might not be aware that Yeats's understanding of Eastern cultures is quite different from their own. One such concept is *samsara*, which Yeats takes for an eternal life that transcends death in poems such as 'Mohini Chatterjee', 'Byzantium', 'Sailing to Byzantium' and 'Lapis Lazuli'. But in Buddhism, *samsara* stands for the endless cycle of life and death that one must transcend in order to acquire eternity. Fu further points out that, though only one poem, 'Lapis Lazuli', directly deals with Chinese culture, Yeats benefits more than usually believed from what he learned about Chinese culture through Ezra Pound. In other recent studies, Jerusha McCormack shows, in an essay from 2007 (and subsequent articles), how the ancient Chinese philosopher Zhuangzi (369 BCE–286 BCE), played a crucial role in helping Oscar Wilde formulate his literary aesthetic.

In addition, consistent efforts have been made to investigate the many literary affinities between Lu Xun and James Joyce, as well as between Yeats and such first-generation modern Chinese poets as Mu Dan (1918–77), Bian Zhiling (1910–2000) and Yuan Kejia (1921–2008), revealing inspirational details that help us to understand those literary figures from comparative perspectives.

Recent Developments

After the People's Republic of China was founded in 1949, particular Irish writers, such as Jonathan Swift and Bernard Shaw, were granted a new and warm reception in China for their vehement social criticism together with a demonstrable sympathy towards the working class. Inspired by Karl Marx's and Friedrich Engels's comments on the cause of Irish independence as part of the international struggle of the working class against the bourgeoisie, Chinese scholars translated into Mandarin in 1974 the first modern book on Irish history, Edmund Curtis's *A History of Ireland* (1936).

The second notable period of China's flourishing interest in Irish Studies in general and Irish literature in particular emerged from quite a different context. Since the mid-1990s, the economic success of Ireland as the 'Celtic Tiger' coincided with a revival of all genres of literature in Ireland – in what has been called a 'second renaissance' of Irish writing. Consistent efforts by the Irish government and cultural institutions, as well as the vast population of Irish emigrants around the world, have made this national literary flowering a global phenomenon. Meanwhile, a rapidly globalized China has been eager to achieve not just economic success but also acknowledged literary expression on the world stage, as finally occurred when Mo Yan (1955–) was awarded the 2012 Nobel Prize in Literature – the first of its kind to a native Chinese writer. In this achievement, Ireland may be said to have provided a model.

But such tangible changes occurred only after the opening up of China and the establishment of diplomatic relationships in 1979 between Ireland and China. Along with the rapid institutional development of Chinese universities, Irish Studies has gradually developed into an acknowledged academic field with several Irish Studies centres and programmes established in the last decade. Currently there are Irish Studies centres at Beijing Foreign Studies University (BFSU), Nanjing University, Shanghai Normal University, Shanghai University of International Business and Economics, together with a British and Irish Literature Centre at Hunan Normal University, among others.

Beijing Foreign Studies University, in particular, has had a long tradition of Irish Studies. Far back in the early 1980s, Wang Zuoliang (1916–95) established a Celtic literature section at the BFSU Institute of Foreign Literature. Chen Shu (1937–2017) was among the first Chinese scholars to visit Ireland in the early 1980s. In 2007, the Irish Studies Centre at BFSU was officially established, making it the first and so far the only multidisciplinary research institution in Irish Studies in China. Thanks to the joint efforts of several important forces – including the governments of both sides, BFSU, NUI Maynooth, University College Dublin, University College Cork and Trinity College Dublin – the Centre has achieved rapid growth in subsequent years. Well-known Irish scholars and writers – such as Margaret Kelleher, Dermot Keogh, and Jerusha McCormack – have taught courses for the Centre, often supplemented by seminars and talks by such distinguished guests as Sebastian Barry, Dermot Bolger, Paddy Bushe, Desmond Egan, Hugo Hamilton, Deirdre Madden and Colm Tóibín.

Today the BFSU Irish Studies Centre offers graduate programmes and enrols students on a biennial basis to pursue their MA degrees either in Irish Literature and Culture or in Irish Politics and Economy. One-year courses teaching the Irish language have been introduced since 2010, open to both undergraduates and MA students. As of 2016, student-exchange programmes have also been initiated between BFSU and Ireland's two best-known universities, Trinity College, Dublin

(TCD), and University College, Dublin (UCD), with the assistance of both Irish and Chinese government-funded scholarships. In the first of these, in June 2018, a candidate from the BFSU Centre was announced to have successfully applied for a PhD scholarship jointly funded by UCD and the China Scholarship Council to further her studies at UCD – marking the beginning of a new close cooperation between the two institutions in the field of high-quality research training.

In another initiative, partially funded by the Irish Department of Foreign Affairs and Trade, the Irish Studies centres in China jointly set up the Irish Studies Network in China in March 2014 to promote academic exchanges and cooperation across China. As part of these networking efforts, a series of cultural and academic events have been organized by member centres. For example, an international symposium on 'Literature, Culture and Nation Building in Twentieth-Century Ireland' was held at BFSU in 2014, and one on 'Celtic Literature and Culture in Ireland' at Shanghai University of International Business and Economics in the same year. Shanghai Normal University holds an annual academic salon to commemorate Irish writers, including W. B. Yeats (2015), Brian Friel (2016) and John Millington Synge (2017). On 15–17 June 2018, scholars from various centres met in Shanghai to celebrate Bloomsday and to discuss issues concerning the network under the rubric of Irish Studies in China. Now with the fortieth anniversary of diplomatic ties between China and Ireland approaching, further events are being planned to celebrate the occasion: among them, the publication of this book.

Apart from explicitly designated courses, major Irish writers such as Beckett, Joyce, Shaw, Swift, Wilde and Yeats are being routinely taught in the English departments of most Chinese universities, though frequently under the umbrella title of English Literature or British Literature. Such courses reinforce the impact of Irish Studies in China, since professors and students soon discover that literary texts are inseparable from their social and historical contexts. To understand those writers better, they will find they need to learn more about Ireland.

Tao looking through the Radcliffe Telescope in University College London Observatory at Mill Hill, c. 1960. The telescope is still in use. Courtesy of the Kiang family.

Tao Kiang with wife Trudi, children and grandchildren on the occasion of his eightieth birthday in 2009. Courtesy of the Kiang family.

Green Dragon dance for Dublin Chinese New Year celebrations, 2018.
© *The Irish Times*.

A 2015 poster for *The Beauty Queen of Leenane*. Courtesy of Drum Tower West Theatre, Beijing.

A poster for Bloomsday celebrations in Shanghai 2017, imagining the Chinese reader's response to translations of Joyce's *Ulysses*. Courtesy of Rob Berry.

One of several posters displayed in the Shanghai Metro system as part of the international Yeats2015 celebrations. Courtesy of the National Library of Ireland.

A Chinese man points near a large billboard advertising the translation of James Joyce's *Finnegans Wake* on a street in Beijing, 30 January, 2013. © Ng Han Guan/AP/Shutterstock.

Chinese translation of *Finnegans Wake* showing varied print format. Courtesy of Shanghai People's Publishing House (上海人民出版社).

Beer mat from Finnegans Wake Irish Bar in Nanjing.

Riverdance company at the Great Wall, 2003. Courtesy of Abhann
Productions.

Riverdance's new dancing style. Courtesy of Abhann Productions.

The Flamenco interlude. Courtesy of Abhann Productions.

Trading Taps: an instance of cross-cultural transmission. Courtesy of Abhann Productions.

The then Vice-President Xi Jinping of China and former Minister for Agriculture, Simon Coveney, visiting the farm of James Lynch in Sixmilebridge, County Clare, 2012. © Maxwell Photography/PA Wire.

Jiuzhaiguo National Park, Sichuan, in autumn.
© THONGCHAI S/Shutterstock.

Publications

Irish literature has long been the mainstream subject of Irish Studies in China, though great progress has been made in recent years in developing other fields beyond literature. The impetus for this development has been provided by translations of Irish literary works, now comprising a major portion of publications in this field.

At the top of the list for translators and publishers are major works of major writers such as Beckett, Joyce, Shaw, Wilde and Yeats, with usually more than one translated version of their major works. Recent notable achievements include the translations of Joyce's *Ulysses* and *Finnegans Wake*, along with *The Complete Works of Samuel Beckett*.

The translation of *Ulysses* in particular caused a sensation in Chinese academia in the 1990s, not only because it is such a challenging book to read and translate, but also because two independent versions, both from renowned Chinese translators, were published within a short interval. Xiao Qian (1910–99) and his wife Wen Jieruo (1927–) published their Mandarin translation of the first volume of *Ulysses* with Yilin Press in April 1994, and then the whole book in October 1994. Jin Di (1921–2008), a well-known Joyce researcher and translator, initially published the first volume of *Ulysses* in traditional Chinese characters with Taiwan's Chiu Ko Publishing Company in 1993, before publishing the whole book in a Mandarin version with the People's Literature Publishing House in 1996. Perhaps an even more remarkable 'mission impossible' was achieved by Dai Congrong, whose Mandarin translation of *Finnegans Wake* was published by Shanghai People's Publishing House in 2012, with the eight thousand copies of the first edition sold out within three weeks (see her essay in this book on this heroic feat). From 2012 to 2015, Shanghai Translation Publishing House also published the *Selected Works of James Joyce* in seven volumes, including *Letters*, *Critical Writings* and *Essays*, in addition to *Dubliners*, *Portrait of the Artist as a Young Man*, and other frequently anthologized works.

Finally, Hunan Literature and Art Publishing House published in 2016 *The Complete Works of Samuel Beckett* as a way to pay tribute to the great author on the occasion of the 110th anniversary of his birth. Altogether the whole series contains twenty-two volumes of translated

Beckett's works, covering all the poems, novels, short stories, plays and literary criticism by the Nobel laureate – thus making it the most inclusive anthology of Beckett's works from around the world.

Apart from these by now iconic writers, contemporary Irish literature has also been closely followed and subsequently translated in China. Important awards or events are promptly reported. Reading tours of visiting Irish writers around major Chinese cities, mainly sponsored by the Irish Embassy in China around St Patrick's Day every year, greatly help to promote the popularity of contemporary works among Chinese readers. Meanwhile, a growing reading market that is well-exposed to Western literature further reinforces the already existing interest in Ireland's new writing. Writers such as John Banville, Sebastian Barry, Marina Carr, Anne Enright, Colum McCann, Martin McDonagh, Colm Tóibín and William Trevor are all well-translated and well-read in China.

At the same time, as theatre-going begins to attract China's emerging middle class, Irish contemporary drama, a flowering that has been well acknowledged in the Western world, has also found its way to China's stage. Some of these are performed in English, although more are performed in translated versions to attract a larger audience. Besides canonical works like Beckett's *Waiting for Godot*, contemporary plays – Brian Friel's *Lovers*, McDonagh's *The Beauty Queen of Leenane* and *The Pillowman,* for instance – currently form part of the core repertoire of several art theatres in Beijing and Shanghai. Experiments are also being made with diverse ways of cooperation between the two countries in this field. In 2016, as part of the programmes to celebrate China's Spring Festival, Chinese performers from Chengdu Associated Theatre went to Ireland to tour performances of *The Seagull and Other Birds*, a drama based on Anton Chekhov's original play *The Seagull*. Directed by Gavin Quinn, this version was first performed during the 2014 Dublin Theatre Festival with an Irish cast from Pan Pan Theatre.

As for research publications, there has also been a marked upsurge since the 1990s, marking the emergence of Irish Studies as a distinctive academic field in China's universities. In common with their translations, major works of major writers still remain a focus of attention for most scholars, while others are concentrating on the more contemporary literary landscape in Ireland. Among the big names, Beckett, Joyce, Wilde and Yeats remain the most heavily researched Irish writers in China. Some recent examples might be Dai Congrong's *Book of Freedom: A Reading of Joyce's Finnegans Wake* (2007), Wang Yu's *The Dramatic Narrative in Yeats's Lyrics of the Middle Period* (2014), Shi Qingjing's *Samuel Beckett on the Chinese Stage: 1964–2011* (2015) and Cao Bo's *A Study of Samuel Beckett's Novels of 'Failure'* (2015).

Yet, in tandem with these developments, research interest has also been expanding fast beyond major writers. Chen Li's *Rose upon the Rood of Time: The Twentieth-Century Irish Big-House Novel* (2009) and *Self-Fashioning in the Irish Literary Revival* (2016), Li Chengjian's *A Study of Contemporary Irish Drama* (2015) and Tian Ju's *A Century's Echo of the Irish Dramatic Movement in China* (2017) are some examples.

Besides the surge in literary translations and scholarly research, other fields of Irish Studies, such as history, religion and political science, have also witnessed rapid growth in the past decade. Robert Kee's *Ireland: A History* and Dermot Keogh's *Twentieth-Century Ireland* were translated and published in 2010 and 2017 respectively. The year 2016 witnessed the publication of two translated biographies: *Roy Keane: The Second Half* by Roddy Doyle and Roy Keane, and *James Joyce* by Richard Ellmann (the juxtaposition of these two names might give some insight into the Chinese perception of modern Ireland!). Two pioneering collections, *China and the Irish* (Jerusha McCormack, ed., English version 2009; Chinese version 2010) and *Sino-Irish Relations: Cross-Cultural Perspectives* (Wang Zhanpeng, ed., 2011) have focused on new perspectives provoked by bilateral relationships between China and Ireland.

Besides such translations and research monographs, journal articles and dissertations are also surging in all fields of Irish Studies. Though there are still no titles specially dedicated to Irish Studies in China, leading journals such as *Foreign Literature Review, Foreign Literature, Contemporary Foreign Literature, Chinese Journal of European Studies, The Journal of International Studies* and *Historical Research* are today paying close attention to the latest developments in Irish Studies both within and beyond China.

This scholarly interest has also resulted in the compiling of textbooks specially designed for Chinese students of Irish Studies.

When Professor Jerusha McCormack wrote four chapters on 'Ireland: History, Politics, Government and Culture' in 2005, it was the first time the Republic of Ireland had been included in a standard work for middle school and undergraduate students under the title of *The Society and Culture of Major English-Speaking Countries* (Higher Education Press, Beijing, China, 2005, revised 2010, 2017). Considering that most Chinese people then regarded the Republic of Ireland as a province of the United Kingdom, to have Ireland now branded as a 'major English-speaking country' itself marked a watershed in Chinese-Irish relations.

As for Irish writing, Professor Chen Shu's *An Anthology of Irish Literature* (2004) and *Irish Literature* (2000) are among the most representative publications in this field. The former is an anthology of selected pieces in English by forty-five Irish writers with succinct introductions to each. Those selections, ranging from the end of the seventeenth century to the contemporary era, are designed to give students a comprehensive encounter with the original texts of great Irish works. The latter publication is a literary history in Chinese of both Celtic literature and Irish literature in English. The first part consists of three sections covering Celtic literature from the fifth to the seventeenth centuries. The second consists of ten chapters introducing the main phases of Irish literature in English from the seventeenth century to the present.

Due to the Irish Diaspora and Ireland's increasing prominence in the world, Irish Studies has recently become a distinctly globalized phenomenon. Yet despite that, as my own academic encounters have proved, China still seems to many an unlikely place for Irish Studies, perhaps due to its huge difference in size or its vast distance from Ireland. But there is more common ground between the two countries than one might expect. And however unlikely it appears to be, the seed of Irish Studies has grown into a robust sapling in China, ready now to branch out through further cooperation and fruitful exchanges with its many counterparts around the world.

What seems lacking now is movement the other way around: a reciprocity in getting the research achievements of Chinese scholars translated and published internationally as well as involving them more intensely in international academic exchanges and cooperation.

Chinese scholars have already started to make efforts in this respect, as this article bears testimony. The 2017 IASIL (International Association for the Study of Irish Literatures) Conference held in Singapore, the first of this century to be held in Asia, saw an unusually large group of Asian scholars in general and Chinese scholars in particular. Those of us who attended greeted the occasion as yet more evidence of the ever-increasing interest on both sides of the world in strengthening academic ties between Asian and Western scholars, teachers and students – and all those engaged in the fruitful exchange of ideas between our two republics.

Irish Literature, James Joyce – and Me

Dai Congrong

It has been now over two decades since I began to follow the emergence of James Joyce in China. At first, he seemed quite obscure. Even in the 1990s, Irish literature was still regarded as a part of English literature. As late as 1996, a professor at Peking University questioned my doctoral dissertation for listing William Butler Yeats and Oscar Wilde as Irish writers. Understandably, in such a context, it was quite natural to begin my reading of Irish literature as English literature. However, Irish literature per se attracted me for having so many distinguished modern writers, among them four winners of the Nobel Prize for Literature: W. B. Yeats, George Bernard Shaw, Samuel Beckett and Seamus Heaney – as well as equally great writers such as Jonathan Swift, Laurence Sterne, Oscar Wilde and, of course, James Joyce.

There are countries with as many or even greater writers: America, France, Germany, Russia, the United Kingdom and so forth. Why should Ireland be more attractive? First of all, because its small size and population means that there is a higher percentage of great writers. Secondly, because many of the Irish writers now famous in China appeared in the same modern period, giving their work a significant role in creating an understanding of modern literature. It also struck me that, unlike many other countries where a group of writers appearing in the same period demonstrate similar ideas and styles, Irish writers possess styles quite different from each other. Therefore they cannot be understood as one phenomenon or explained with one idea. Also their influence tends to be registered in different areas and in different ways; such diversity and abundance is not merely attractive, but cannot be ignored.

What was the source of this abundant creativity of Irish writers? This question inspired my research and, eventually, my translation of James Joyce. In the beginning, I only intended to find out why Joyce's style is so disconcerting for so many ordinary people (many declare that they cannot finish *Ulysses*) while compelling for readers with a more literary education (in 1998 *Ulysses* came first in a list of best twentieth-century novels in English). This question shaped my PhD dissertation, finally published as *Form Experiments in James Joyce's Texts* and focusing on Joyce's contribution to modern art techniques.

However, the more I read Joyce, the more I realized that this creativity had something to do with Irish culture. It is Irish culture itself that gives Irish writers a wide understanding and acceptance of human life. The resulting complexity and their sharp sensibility makes these writers' representations of modern life moving. I believe that this special breadth and depth comes neither from an ideological or abstract understanding of the nature of life, nor from an understanding of art, but from a heart that embraces this troubled world. Moreover, such a heart cannot survive in a highly hierarchical society under the critical and haughty stare of the gentry. It can exist only in a suffering nation where people can sympathize with those stuck in their inabilities, where people can understand each other's incapability – while still holding on to the hope that a national conscience will one day be forged. It is the heart of Leopold Bloom in Joyce's *Ulysses*. As an ordinary suffering husband and father, he shares his sympathy with others while still holding on to hope of improvement.

In his early works, *Dubliners* and *A Portrait of the Artist as a Young Man*, Joyce tends to be more critical of ordinary Irish people. Stephen Dedalus and Gabriel, stand-ins for the fictional Joyce, keep their distance from their surrounding community. However, Joyce himself changed after he left, with Nora, for the Continent. When Joyce finally found his way into the actual culture of the Irish people, his protagonists changed as well, enabling him to show his sympathy with all sorts of individuals on this diverse and abundant island. Thus Bloom believes that love is the last word, by showing sympathy with the indecent Gerty and poor Ms Purefoy among others. While in *Finnegans Wake*, HCE and Shem – brought low as malefactors and now charged by others – although hurt, still stay with the world they love.

Having arrived at this new understanding, I published my first paper, entitled 'James Joyce and Irish Folk Culture', in a famous Chinese journal. I suggest that it is just this merging into Irish culture and its distinctive spirit that gives *Ulysses* and *Finnegans Wake* the richness and inclusiveness that other works lack. In 2015, a troupe of Irish actors presented *Ulysses* in Shanghai. Their performance demonstrated vividly the atmosphere and spirit of Irish pub life that Joyce describes in his late works. Even more clearly, this drama demonstrated the spiritual paralyses of the drinkers, as well as Joyce's feeling of both empathy and detachment. Joyce's complex feeling towards the denizens of the pub can perhaps best be summarized by Lu Xun's famous sentence: 'anguished at their suffering, angered by their paralyses' ('*ai qi bu xing, nu qi bu zheng*'). It is a kind of critical sympathy, one that both identifies with his characters but refuses to give up on them.

Joyce is often compared with Lu Xun in China – and justly so, since both of them lived in a time when their nations were anguished and awakening. Both writers focused on the 'national character' as one of suffering. Having each undertaken medical studies, both quite independently diagnosed this suffering as paralysis. While Joyce vowed in *A Portrait of the Artist as a Young Man* that he would seek 'to forge in the smithy of my soul the uncreated conscience of my race', Lu Xun decided he should devote his life to healing the spirit of his people instead of healing their bodies. For me, their shared mission became especially clear when my Irish friends told me about the sympathy Irish people felt for Chinese people, both nations having been colonized and exploited for a long time in their respective histories.

★   ★   ★   ★

This new understanding of Irish culture has changed my view of Irish writers and even my understanding of world literature. It has also transformed my attitude towards the society I live in, as I feel myself becoming more kind-hearted towards others after I have read Joyce.

In the case of literature, readers generally equate refined work to good work. In Joyce's time, even writers such as Virginia Woolf preferred this kind of belles-lettres, as artistic beauty is understood as being elegant. Irish writers are completely capable of making this kind of refined literature. For example, Joyce's *A Portrait of the Artist as a Young Man* builds on a delicate structure, its exquisite sentences relating the spiritual life story of an artistic protagonist.

Only after he had finished the draft of *A Portrait* did Joyce come to understand the importance of Irish popular culture – and especially pub culture – possibly due to his marriage with Nora along with a growing sympathy for his father as a kind of pub star. First depicted as a loser in the early story 'Counterparts' in *Dubliners*, by the time Joyce came to write *Ulysses*, his father emerges as Simon Dedalus: a charming dandy, winning the favour of both waitresses and customers with his singing and good humour. When he was young, Joyce hated the drunkards in Irish pubs who reminded him of his father. Not until his later period did Joyce come to embrace the resources of Irish pub culture, in all its goodness and badness. Hence the pub becomes a predominant venue in *Ulysses* – and almost the only venue in *Finnegans Wake*. In that book it becomes the whole universe, as well as the history of human life from the beginning to its next beginning. There all the world's people and every event in the world's history are imagined as their stories are told at an inn: a place popular in Ireland where people live upstairs and share their life in the bar downstairs.

Thus, for Joyce, life itself is performed in an Irish bar, no matter good or bad. There is love too, which, in *Ulysses*, is what Leopold Bloom sticks to. But if the bar is representative of Irish life, it is not the only place. Streets, rivers, homes, libraries and many other places are also mentioned in Joyce's work – in fact, the world is in Joyce's work, with all its goodness and badness. It is said that once James Joyce and Marcel Proust met at a party. However, they did not talk much to each other. When asked why, Joyce said that he and Proust were not interested in each other because Proust was interested in ladies (high society, therefore upholding social standards) while he was interested in maids (servants, from the lower orders, who might feel free to flout them). As his response reveals, Joyce is not only interested in maids, he is interested in the whole of life, high or low. This gives his work unusual breadth and inclusiveness.

Now I can enjoy both inclusive and comprehensive work as well as exclusive and refined work, with only a little preference for the former, which, I believe, can bring me to different ways of seeing things. An inclusive work accepts diversity and demonstrates that in this world there will be a place for everyone. Such a work also accepts ambiguity, believing that people can both be good and bad. Joyce admits that this world is a battlefield, but he also insists that it is a place for love – or, in the words of Mr Dedalus as summarized in *Ulysses*, 'love and war'. As the two basic themes of human life, they coexist in the world. Thus, in his later works, Joyce still describes the underlying struggles between family members, friends and strangers. However, in his vision, the protagonist is not much better than his counterpart. Shem – who is regarded as a devil by others in *Finnegans Wake* – is also a saint, while Shaun – who is regarded as saint by others – is also a devil. Unlike his earlier works, the boundary between good and bad, right and wrong, true and false in his later works is no longer as clear as it once had been.

Easier said than done. To apply this attitude to any description of the world in a novel is not that simple. Only a heart really embracing this world could create such a work. Seamus Heaney, for instance, suffered between conflicting statuses for a long time: such as being loyal to one's nation as opposed to being loyal to oneself, being attached to life as against being willing to die, being dedicated to art as against social responsibility. In 1972 he moved from Belfast to the Republic of Ireland. After that, Heaney seemed to accept more and more an attitude of living 'in between'. This 'in between' not only gave him a free space as well as an open mind; it also gave his late poems a broad vision, which moves more naturally between common things and spiritual meditation, between Ireland and the outside world. It also gave him an acceptance of diversity and inclusiveness that he shares with Joyce and many other Irish writers. This inclusiveness climaxes in his last work, *Human Chain*. Traditionally, a human chain is a form of public demonstration in which people link their arms as a show of political solidarity. It is a gesture to demonstrate the sympathy between people with the same purpose. Seamus Heaney uses the metaphor of the human chain first to indicate the integral linkage between the past and the present, between himself and his ancestors. However, he also uses it to describe the linkage between all human beings, between himself and others. As his friend Sean O'Brien said, in these poems Heaney 'speaks to us like an adult addressing other adults, who must, like him, remember innocence and encompass loss'.[1]

This human chain even exists beyond human beings – as between human beings and other existences. In 'A Herbal', a sequence of nineteen short poems, Heaney describes these plants in a commentary that becomes a meditation on death, rupture and inheritance, as human beings are bound into the larger background of the natural world. Interestingly, the herbs are even credited with having different human characteristics. Some are noble and some are low; some are kind and some are malignant. However, even one as low as broom can still be company; and even one as vicious as nettles can still teach us tolerance. Besides, 'There would always be dock leaves / To cure the vicious stings'. If the coarse frogs in his first poetry collection, *The Death of a Naturalist*, make the young Heaney sicken, turn and run, now, in his last poetry collection, the natural world to him is 'like a nest / Of crosshatched grass blades' where he exists in 'between'. His attitude changes completely when Heaney opens himself more and more to his native Irish culture, traditionally immersed in the natural realm. It is this aspect of Irish culture – its ability to open itself to the larger world – that moves me most.

With this new appreciation of the inclusiveness of Irish culture, I began my translation of *Finnegans Wake*. This is why I decided to keep the multiple meanings, the complexity and the possibility of including every related history and culture in *Finnegans Wake* as much as I could.

However, even though I was aware that Joyce had put serious consideration into inventing portmanteau words for *Finnegans Wake*, when I began my translation, I could not help but regard many of them as somehow unnecessary or misprinted. So I left possible meanings out when I thought them unrelated to the main narrative. One day, when I translated 'one yeastyday he sternely struxk his tete in a tub for to watsch the future of his fates but ere he swiftly stook it out again, by the might of moses, the very water was eviparated and all the guenneses had met their exodus so that ought to show you what a pentschan-jeuchy chap he was!'[2], I suddenly realized how ingeniously different ideas (here the folk song of '*Finnegans Wake*' and the holy story of Exodus) were combined by Joyce. I realized I was translating a book of genius that turns the spirit of inclusive Irish culture into words of the most all-encompassing power. Since then, I decided I had no right to cut *Finnegans Wake* just as I liked and should try instead to retain all the possible meanings, no matter what I thought of the author's intention.

In fact when *Finnegans Wake* was in progress, some friends of James Joyce declared that he was mad or that he was pulling the reader's leg. Even Harriet Shaw Weaver and Ezra Pound, his loyal fans, had doubts about this book. As their support was always important to Joyce, their hesitation rendered him too depressed to write anything for some considerable time. Sensing this hard pressure, his wife, Nora, tried to persuade him to write something a bit less difficult for others. She had never interfered with his writing before. Joyce, however, would not give up this 'cursed' book for no significant reason, even though he felt so demoralized that he complained to friends that his task was certainly as difficult as that of the Creator. But no matter how he struggled, it never occurred to Joyce to give up.

There is no clear record as to why Joyce insisted on writing such an abstruse book. One explanation is that he wished to write a night book with the language of night. Logical language does not belong to the night. This suggestion comes from his younger brother, Stanislaus Joyce, in 1926, at a time when Joyce had already finished book one and most of book three, with the idiosyncratic language we see today. Thus, Stanislaus's declaration is more like an explanation of what had already happened than of his brother's original intention.

It seems that in the beginning Joyce was considering simply rewriting the Irish myth of Roderick O'Conor, the last high king of Ireland who, for Joyce, represented the end of Celtic kingdom. Other materials he collected for this book included 'Tristan and Isolde', 'Saint Patrick and the Druid', 'Kevin's Orisons', 'Mamalujo' and 'Here Comes Everybody'. Saint Patrick, as the patron saint of Ireland, represents its Christian history, just as O'Conor represents the Celtic history of Ireland. The legend of St Kevin, who is said to have lived in fifth-century early-Christian Ireland, relates mostly to animals or the natural world. This combination of the natural and the Christian in St Kevin's story represents a transitional, Celtic–Christian period, in Irish culture. Therefore, it seems that Joyce was preparing to write a book covering the course of Irish antiquity.

However, this was certainly not all of his plan. The 'Mamalujo' theme is an abbreviation of the four gospels of the New Testament: Matthew, Mark, Luke and John. The 'Here Comes Everybody' forms one name, that of the protagonist HCE. HCE is also the abbreviation of 'Haveth Childers Everywhere', 'Howth Castle and Environs', as well as Humphrey Chimpden Earwicker. To give these characters in *Finnegans Wake* both a general and abbreviated name – each including many possibilities – indicates that Joyce was prepared to write about not only Ireland but also the history of the whole world. Joyce himself said that his book is a 'microbemost cosm' (*Finnegans Wake*, p.151) with 'most spacious immensity' (p.150). This also explains why he said that there would be nothing else worth his doing after finishing *Finnegans Wake* – except to die.

To include the whole world and its history in one book makes it as grand, complicated and inclusive as the work of the Creator. Joyce does not simply list the events of human history as if from a history book. Instead, he seeks to represent the spirit of the world as it moves through history, just as he sought the spirit of Irish culture in the pubs of *Ulysses*. What language can reach to being that inclusive, immense and kaleidoscopic ('collideorscape', p.143)? As the language of the whole world and its history, the idiom of *Finnegans Wake* should be more multiple, more ambiguous than other literary language. It should also be inclusive, derivative and transmutable, to include the past and the present, human beings and their entire universe, the known and the unknown. No existing language can do so much. Thus Joyce had to create this language himself. Its words must convey both the vibration of the universe and the breath of history. For Joyce, a word must create a world.

★ ★ ★ ★

Finnegans Wake began to attract serious attention from Chinese readers only in the 1990s, although James Joyce's writing was introduced into China as early as the 1920s. In 1998, Zhenqi Ding limited his discussion of different Chinese translations of *Finnegans Wake* to its title because at that time this book was only mentioned as one of Joyce's works – no one had read it yet. According to Ding, the Chinese title should be something like 'The Record of the Changing World'. This belongs to a Chinese title tradition that places it in a category similar to that of *Gulliver's Travels*, indicating that his impression of *Finnegans Wake* was that of a realistic story relating the protagonist's changing fortune within the world.[3] Clearly, Ding had not read it either. But now, with the beginning of the twenty-first century, close readings of *Finnegans Wake* are finally occurring in China, with some papers actually discussing the book in detail.

In 2003, I received state funding for *Finnegans Wake* research. In the following four years, I published four papers altogether and, in January 2007, the first and only book on *Finnegans Wake* in China, entitled the *Book of Freedom: Reading Finnegans Wake*.[4] At the same time, the number of those eager to read *Finnegans Wake* has increased year after year. Many people visiting a public website created to allow Chinese readers to make comments on any books that interested them expressed their wish to read a full translation.[5] At that point, not even a chapter of the text had been translated except for some paragraphs in critical books such as *The Western Canon*.[6]

After signing a contract with Shanghai VI HORAE Publishers in 2006, I began my translation of *Finnegans Wake*. Since there are so many meanings and allusions hidden in just one word in *Finnegans Wake*, I did not wish to publish too simple a translation by choosing only one or two meanings for Joyce's words, as this would be hopelessly superficial and would mislead – maybe even disillusion – Chinese readers. For me, *Finnegans Wake* is like a poem, whose meaning comes not just from the denotations of every word but from the very structures and rhythms they build, the narratives and styles they assume, as well as the images and senses they convey. When translating this kind of work, some dimensions are, of course, bound to be lost. My solution is to include only one of many possible meanings in the main text. Other meanings are in footnotes, a section extending to sometimes twice the size of the text's main body. As to which meaning to choose, the more I translated, the more I found there was a kind of logical relation between adjacent sentences – allowing me to build my main text on the basis of it. In this way, I believe I have given Chinese readers an interconnected narrative, one which will make *Finnegans Wake* readable and even attractive to its public.

In my translation the footnotes – indispensable in the effort to help readers understand the rich dimensions of *Finnegans Wake* – are no less important than the main text. In these footnotes I put all the possible meanings and hidden words the Joyceans and I have been able to decipher. Since English is highly popular among literate Chinese people, in each footnote I used the original *Finnegans Wake* words as well as similar words in Latin alongside their Chinese translations. Were only Chinese words presented, the footnotes might look pretentious or whimsical. By thus including original words and synonyms, some Chinese readers might be able to comprehend Joyce's combination of different words into one (i.e., his famous portmanteau expressions) and thus have a deeper understanding of the uncertainty, changeability and multiplicity of *Finnegans Wake*.

The sentences in Joyce's *Finnegans Wake* do not follow the standard rules of syntax either. Joyce created this type of irregular sentence to give his readers a more flexible and open understanding of the way language can suggest multiple meanings. However, in the beginning, I dared not translate the text into sentences that were too ungrammatical, fearing the critique of Chinese readers. Instead, I chose the most logical one to make the sentences look grammatical.

However, as I translated more and more sentences, becoming increasingly at ease with his ungrammatical approach, I became braver in rendering such sentences in a way that helped create poly-meanings and even, ultimately, uncertain meanings. For example, 'Bygmester

Finnegan, of the Stuttering Hand' (*Finnegans Wake*, p. 4) was translated as 'Big master Finnegan, of stammering hand' to reflect the original quote. 'Stuttering' has both the meaning of 'shaking' and 'stammering', but to translate 'stuttering' as 'stammering' instead of 'shaking' would force Chinese readers to find the similarity between the protagonist HCE and Irish politician Charles Stewart Parnell, the English writer Lewis Carroll, as well as between Aesop, Aristotle, Moses, Isaac Newton, etc. ('etc.' being the writing rule of *Finnegans Wake* in which every word there can include more possibilities than can be listed or found) – all of whom were stammerers and act as models for HCE's other personalities.

Unruly words and sentences were often used by Joyce to force his readers into a more open, complex and inclusive mindset. A standard translation would therefore work against his purpose, as it would lose the richness in his book and bring readers back into the hierarchical world. I realized that illogical sentences – disobeying standard grammar – and apparently scrambled words are speech acts (as Raymond Federman demonstrates in his *Take It or Leave It*) that work against the orthodox language of the elite. Just as traditional grammar, which places subject, verb and predicate in a hierarchical order, will lead readers to accept a hierarchical structure as natural, a free book demands unruly words and sentences in order to free readers from this traditional mental structure.

However, for a culture which respects long-standing tradition, such as the Chinese, a completely unorthodox translation would set too many challenges for its readers, taking the risk of losing their respect. This is one reason I chose a format similar to the format of many ancient Chinese classics. This kind of format is used in particular in expository writings on the Confucian classics, called the '*Zhu-shu* version'. It consists of three parts: 1) the original text printed in a large font; 2) the explanation or commentary printed in a medium font following the original word or sentence to be explained; 3) a detailed explanation printed in a smaller font and put into two lines immediately after the first explanation. My Chinese translation of *Finnegans Wake* adopted this format with a slight variation. It also contains three parts: 1) the main translated text printed in a large font on the left page, selecting a meaning from the many alternatives and put into somewhat logical sentences; 2) other possible meanings following immediately after the word to be explained in the main text, printed in a medium font; 3) more detailed explanations of ambiguous words and allusions in the original or its translation, placed on the right-hand page.

The similarity between the two formats, one ancient and one modern, gives the Chinese reader of *Finnegans Wake* a sense of the long tradition of the *Zhu-shu* version, implying that Joyce's book is also to be highly respected and much researched. It also implies the existence of an 'industry' surrounding the text and that this industry has a stronger relation to serious academic research than to the event-targeting media. Finally, it implies that the text carries a profound, enlightening knowledge to which literate readers must devote time. With this format, the Chinese translation has now found a balance between the orthodox and unorthodox, between following and breaking with tradition. Here, within its pages, is the kind of inclusiveness and diversity that I have learnt from Irish culture.

Finnegans Wake is a small book but it opens a reader to the whole world and its history. To me, Ireland is also a small Ireland but open to the whole world and its history; thus, for me, making *Finnegans Wake* its one true book.

Endnotes

1   O'Brien, Sean (2010), 'Human Chain, by Seamus Heaney', *Irish Independent*, 2 September.
2   James Joyce. *Finnegans Wake*. New York: Viking Press, 1939, p. 4, lines 21–25. All further references are to this text.
3   Ding, Zhenqi (1998), 'Translations of the Title of *Finnegans Wake*', *Journal of WuXi Normal College*, vol. 1, p. 43.
4   Dai, Congrong (2007), *Book of Freedom: Reading Finnegans Wake*. Shanghai: Press of East China Normal University.
5   See http://book.douban.com/subject/1949780/.
6   Bloom, Harold (2005), *The Western Canon*, trans. Ningkang Jiang. Nanjing: Yilin Press, pp. 336–40.

A *Riverdance* for China

Guo Ruxin and Liu Hongchi

Melodious violins, vicissitudes of the Irish pipes, thick drums, an ethereal singer and a dancing beat that people cannot help but follow were all mixed up together. The hard dance shoe was like a dancer's musical instrument, the dancer expressing both joy and sorrow while being on the beat. This was *Riverdance*, a visual carnival and an auditory feast.

Riverdance Past and Present

The birth of *Riverdance* started with a unique opportunity. In 1994 the predecessor of *Riverdance* was performed on the screen as a seven-minute interlude for the Eurovision Song Contest: worldwide, the largest competition in TV history. Michael Flatley, an Irish–American choreographer, and his dancing partner Jean Butler shocked their audience with their boldly innovative style. Unlike traditional Irish dancing, they did not pay attention to movements of only the lower limbs while holding the upper body stiff. Instead they introduced a new kind of seductive choreography, with an enhanced visual appeal, a strengthening rhythm and a larger, more expressive body range. These innovations, together with the high-pitched and impassioned music created by Irish composer Bill Whelan, won over the crowd.

Overnight, *Riverdance* became a sensation. With the enthusiastic response of 300 million European audience members behind them, the creators decided to expand it into a large-scale work. By the following year, *Riverdance*, with new choreography drawing on Irish themes in a grand, dramatic narrative, was staged in Dublin and later the same year in London. Even with critical London audiences, *Riverdance* proved a wild success, the only negativity coming from those established music and dance diehards who decided that *Riverdance* spelled the death knell for traditional arts. (In fact, the opposite happened, with *Riverdance* giving the tradition a much-needed shot in the arm.)

These critics also might have been taken aback at the initial structure of the show, one that had been determined at the very start of rehearsals. It was at this early stage that John McColgan, Bill Whelan and Moya Doherty decided to move beyond a merely Irish dance show into a larger world context, integrating into its choreography such diverse dance traditions as Spanish flamenco, American tap and Russian Slavic dancing. All these elements were retained with only small-scale modifications over the next five years: these numbers moved from Act One to Act Two (and sometimes back again), some new numbers were introduced and others later withdrawn, according to the year and the context of the tour.

In 2000, *Riverdance* officially entered Broadway. At that point, and after many years of reorganization and innovation, its repertoire and narrative structure had become increasingly stable. As Julian Erskine, the production executive, observed, 'For the first five years of the show many modifications were made to content and running order, but the core items of the show remained intact; so, by the time we got to Broadway the touring shows were set and have remained largely unchanged ever since.'

Riverdance in China

In October 2003 *Riverdance* was introduced into China. As the closing show of the first Beijing International Drama Performance season, *Riverdance* played six consecutive gigs in the Great Hall of the People in Beijing. Afterwards, *Riverdance* was brought to Shanghai; as the opening performance of the fifth Shanghai International Arts Festival, it played in five consecutive sessions for the Shanghai Grand Stage. At this time, China's performance market was still in its primary stage of development. Although it was already enjoying a remarkable reputation

in the rest of the world, when *Riverdance* came to China for the first time, a more muted response was expected. But in fact the ticketing data show that, in Beijing at least, *Riverdance* actually broke the box office record of the time for the Great Hall of the People.

As is well known, 2008 – the year in which China hosted the Olympic Games – was an unforgettable one for the Chinese people. In that year *Riverdance* came to China again. As an important project of the official 2008 Olympic Cultural Activities, it gave eight consecutive performances in the National Centre for the Performing Arts in Beijing and a further eight performances in Xian. Owing to its own artistic quality as well as to the excitement generated by the Olympic Games, *Riverdance* created another box office record, this time for the National Centre for the Performing Arts.

But it was the 2009 Chinese Central TV Spring Festival Gala Evening that finally transported *Riverdance* into the homes of millions of Chinese families. There is no doubt that watching the Spring Festival Gala has become, since 1983, year after year, an essential part of the Chinese people's New Year's Eve celebrations. As an annual spectacle, Chinese television directors often mobilize various means to arrange splendid programmes in different forms in order to meet the aesthetic needs of audiences at different levels. Thus, in 2009, *Riverdance* was introduced as a fresh element, its vigorous dancing and kicking pace creating a sensation. Although regarded as quite exotic, this 'audible dance' aroused the collective feelings of Chinese people. The '*Riverdance* effect', as it was called, belonging specifically to China, had officially kicked off.

Why Is *Riverdance* So Popular in China?

Undoubtedly, as a comprehensive art, *Riverdance* integrated the three elements of dance presentation, singing and instrumental performance perfectly. People may ask, 'Well, what is *Riverdance*? Is it a dance drama, a musical drama, or a song and dance drama?' Admittedly, it is still difficult for us to define, but its combination of a long-established culture with an exploration of new artistic ideas makes *Riverdance* a model of contemporary art. Here are a few considerations of elements that made it particularly popular with Chinese audiences.

Riverdance as a Unique Phenomenon

The uniqueness of *Riverdance*, now twenty-five years on the stage, resides in its innovation of otherwise traditional modes. Unlike some operas and ballets, which are performed only for certain audiences, *Riverdance* sought to reach people from all walks of life. In order to construct a cross-class cultural and ethnic identity, it became necessary to break through the boundaries of social class or strata and merge or even mix distinctions.

In the presentation of an Irish dance vocabulary, vulgarity and elegance became the same as each other, and the dances of social elites and the folk were transformed into something new and arresting. In other words, for its Chinese audience, *Riverdance* broke through people's expectations of what it means to be an artistic 'work'. While we in China often admire the art of the classics and the stage, we habitually oppose the relationships between seriousness and entertainment, elegance and popularity. For us, it is surprising that a cultural work with serious themes can also be entertaining. Admittedly, the Irish epic carried by *Riverdance* appears heavy, but its main expressive carrier – the Irish step dance – is itself light.

It should, however, be distinguished from tap dance, developed over more than a hundred years from many different sources: evolving from African tribal dancing and traditional Irish and Scottish step dances such as the hornpipe and the jig. One might argue that both styles of hard-shoe dancing originated from separate rebellions against political power. Irish traditional step dancing – a relatively antique form – was practised surreptitiously by the Irish, even though banned by the British colonialists, while American tap developed from the struggle between blacks and whites as blacks moved into the cities during the long process of urbanization in the new world.

Both of these styles are present in *Riverdance*. While traditional Irish dance provided the driving force and American tap an auxiliary one, they are made to collide with each other. In Act Twelve, 'The Harbour of a New World', one can see this collision taking place as white people compete with black people, each in their own dance style. In terms of this style, the Irish dancers tend to perform with a tall and straight upper body accompanied by a more staid and formal rhythm while the American black dancers perform in a looser style, displaying a fresh confidence along with a kind of cynical humour. In the course of the dance sequence, each learns from the other, beginning to mix steps through a unique dialogue in which the competing folk styles are expounded vividly and incisively.

It is worth mentioning that, although traditional Irish dancing once tended to be open in form and simple and loose in style, it went underground when laws were introduced under British colonization in the 1600s to suppress Irish music and dance. In the late 1800s, during the Celtic revival, when traditional dancing was brought back, its style had changed. By the late 1920s, in a concerted drive to reintroduce traditional Irish dance to the burgeoning Irish Republic, dance competitions were set up to encourage young dancers. This new style of competitive dancing then became the norm: it involved stern faces along with a stiff carriage of the upper body – as the judges wanted to see only the artistry of the feet and nothing else. In 1995 *Riverdance* freed Irish dance from the rigid rules and costumes of these competitions forever. Its freer style of dance encouraged the dancers to smile, move their whole bodies more freely and actively entertain the audience. Interestingly, this looser style of dance is actually much closer to the original pre-competitive Irish dance known as *Sean Nós* (old style).

Ironically, perhaps, in invoking this older style, *Riverdance* has evolved into something more in line with the contemporary audience's aesthetics. Here upper limbs have a more flexible movement; the stony-faced dancers now smile at the audience and at each other; and at the same time, their overall dancing posture is more relaxed, allowing them to open and close according to the storyline. In addition to traditional tiptoe rotation and air strikes, the choreographers also imported the 'A' jump from figure skating, which heightened the routine's excitement.

It is important, too, to note that *Riverdance*, although an important Irish cultural symbol, avoided being stuck in narrow nationalism by opening itself to a diversity of different forms of traditional dancing from around the world. Through this innovation, a certain monotony of style was averted while at the same time enhancing the dance's ornamental value. On the other hand, the collision and integration of such 'cross-culture' art has elicited some unexpected reactions, as Spanish flamenco, American jazz and Russian Slavic dance have each become indispensable cultural features in *Riverdance*. For example, in Act Six, 'Fire Dance', the interval of Spanish flamenco shocked the Chinese audience. As the dancer's red skirt seemed to catch fire from the scorching sun filling the sky, her bold and wild dancing posture blazed with sexual energy. In contrast, Act Three, 'Countess Cathleen', appeared grand and solemn – inspired by the Irish poet Yeats's play of the same name, which was itself a great sensation when first put on the stage in Dublin. In the play, Cathleen sells her soul to the devil to save her compatriots from famine; when she finally goes to heaven, she is regarded as a symbol of Ireland's maternal image. In the *Riverdance* sequence, the dancing style invokes elements of graceful modern ballet to express Cathleen's feminine beauty while using forceful hard-shoe dance steps to show how the strength possessed by men is challenged by the independence and tenacity of women. In this way, *Riverdance* seeks to represent the Countess Cathleen as a metaphor for the rise of the Irish nation.

Yet, as these sequences are themselves disconnected, *Riverdance* does not adhere rigidly to the attributes of the dance drama. Thus it is probably better to think of it as a combination of dance performance, singing and instrumental music that varies in different passages with different emphases. For example, in Act Two, 'The Heart's Cry', the unaccompanied chorus is quiet and beautiful, with an ethereal voice that seems to come from the deep, chanting the natural longing of the human's spiritual search. In Act Four, the 'Caoineadh Chu Chullainn' ('Lament for Cuchulainn'), an elegy is played for probably the greatest warrior hero of Irish mythology. Performed by a lone piper at sunset, the sound is uniquely Irish. For the pipes used in *Riverdance* are not in fact bagpipes (which are Scottish) but the traditional uilleann pipes (*uilleann* being the Irish word for 'elbow', as the air is pumped through the pipes by the motion of the piper's elbow). In contrast to the loud, often raucous sound of the bagpipes – used by the Scots in warfare – the uilleann pipes have a softer, plangent resonance that amplifies the sadness of its slow airs.

Following this slow lament, Act Five, 'Thunderstorm', comes as a shock, with dozens of the male actors standing in the midst of thunder and the lightning's flash. Whether or not this scene is a reference to the eventual uprising of the Irish people against the English – its precise pace sustained by strong and powerful foot drumming – it can also be interpreted as a symbol of how, even in the face of natural disasters, people anywhere in the world will never give up.

Finally, in the form of its actual performance, *Riverdance* once again challenges the audience's expectations as, in many ways, it is not presented as a traditional artistic work. For instance, there are no rules to oblige the spectators to be serious in speech and manners. We can cheer, we can stamp our feet, we can even stand up and dance in time to the performance. In the thousands of actual performances that one might see, *Riverdance* is one of the few during which people can take pictures and record videos on their phones and also 'shake their heads along'. Dancers can 'talk' on stage and we in the audience can 'interact' with them. When this occurs, many spectators might have the illusion that the dancers were not on the stage or that we were on stage with them. The live orchestral music makes such audience immersion even more intense. It is the 'liveliness' of *Riverdance* that makes every performance of it inimitable.

The Role of Modern Media

In addition to appreciating *Riverdance*'s artistic value, the makers of *Riverdance* have also understood the crucial role of modern marketing. As an anti-traditional form of performance (that is, serious performance reinterpreted as entertainment), the promotion of *Riverdance* has also been anti-traditional. At the beginning of its run, *Riverdance* subverted the small-scale spread of the artwork in the past. Instead, it adopted a large-scale television-led promotion. The predecessor of *Riverdance* was performed on the screen as an interlude performance for the Eurovision Song Contest, broadcast onscreen through PBS in the US, SKY in the UK, TV Channel 2 in Germany and TV Channel 5 in France. It was also repeated intensively. Although it happened by chance, the repeated TV broadcasts undoubtedly opened the market for *Riverdance*.

After being polished many times, *Riverdance* then played Broadway. There it did not follow the traditional rules of theatre but began to promote DVD recordings at the same time as its live performance. At that time – whether on Broadway in New York or a West End theatre in London – in order to guarantee the box office, a live performance was usually not allowed to be released to the outside world until its run was completed. (This new practice of simultaneous DVD release has now been licensed by other promoters to expand potential audiences.) On this issue, the director, John McColgan, has his own logic: he thinks that everyone who has watched the video of *Riverdance* will become a potential audience for the live performance. And his prediction was certainly confirmed during the following tour.

In the twenty-one years since its first global tour, *Riverdance* has won twenty-one consecutive global box office successes. Its box office is now up to $3 billion (US). It has been performed more than twelve thousand times in the world and, in total, audiences number more than 25 million. In 1997 its stage soundtrack music won the Best Music Album Award at the Grammy Awards. The soundtrack itself has sold more than 11 million copies worldwide: a status of ultra-platinum sales. In terms of live performance, wherever *Riverdance* goes it can be very difficult to get even a single ticket.

In addition to the large number of potential viewers wooed through previous video transmission, its pre-investment costs have also paid off. Taking the performance in China as an example, as early as its first visit to China in 2003, *Riverdance* management devoted considerable resources to publicity and advertising. Before the actual performance, the dance company went twice to Beijing for warm-up productions. During this period, they gave small-scale performances drawing on the highlights of the play. When they came to Shanghai, they even went to colleges and universities to explain and promote their style of Irish dancing to the university students who were intrigued by its novelty. Thus, by placing the promotional activities of *Riverdance* in public places and campuses, they attracted potential audiences into the theatre.

At the end of 2009, *Riverdance* marked its fifteenth anniversary by launching a special edition tour throughout China. With highly organized full pre-publicity – together with the popularity gleaned through the Chinese New Year Gala – they were able to book sixty tours in thirteen cities, with box office sell-outs for every performance.

As the person in charge of the performance of *Riverdance* in China, Li Zhiqiang, said: 'According to the calculation of cost ratio, publicity spending for general performances is at most RMB 7.8 million and there are rarely more than 2 million yuan; but for *Riverdance* this is up to three or four million yuan.' With the help of newspaper, television, radio, Internet and other media reports, as well as various forms of advertising, this tour lasted for one full year.

On 9 February 2010, *Riverdance* as performed at the Beijing Exhibition Centre was recorded again in a special production for China, featuring three Chinese musicians playing the erhu, pipa and bamboo xiao flute. In addition to the performance itself, the DVD on sale also included off-cuts, stills and related reports of the *Riverdance* tour around the country. From that time onwards, as *Riverdance* performances started incorporating certain Chinese nuances and cultural elements, these specific byplays began to spread throughout China and even to the rest of the world. Such exceptional promotional tactics laid a solid foundation for its following annual Chinese tours.

Of course, in addition to the vigorous promotion of its stars, *Riverdance*'s highly elaborate and refined stage and costume design, as well as its excellent artistic quality, have gained many return customers. As some of the senior audiences remarked, 'Those who have never been to see *Riverdance* will never know what they have missed; but those who have seen *Riverdance* will be unable to stop loving it.'

Commonality of World Civilization

Although *Riverdance* purports to tell the story of the Irish nation, it is in fact closely related to the story of every nation. What appears in the plot are common issues of human society, whether these are confrontation with nature, unavoidable wars, or the pain of exile from one's homeland.

In its first half, *Riverdance* focuses on the national origins and folklore of Ireland. The scenery of the God of Forests, originating in Ireland's druidic past, is used many times. In the Act One, 'Reel around the Sun', and Act Six, 'Fire Dance', the dancers' praise of the sun invokes the ancient sun-worship of the Irish people. Act Five, 'Thunderstorm', takes place amidst an onslaught of thunder and lightning through which the dancers stand firm, symbolizing 'humans fighting against nature'. In Act Eight, 'Slip into Spring – The Harvest', the fresh pastoral scenery, embodying its people's hope for the newly fertile land, exemplifies 'the co-existence between man and nature'. Within these scenes, whether it is the worship of sun, mankind's fight against nature, or their necessary co-existence, the emphasis is on a kind of elemental but hidden animism or spiritual connection between the two.

In the second half, *Riverdance* changes the narrative logic by telling how the Irish people, facing both natural calamities and man-made misfortunes, became destitute and homeless, forced into exile. War, famine and slavery severed the original bond between man and nature, disrupting an entire human society and thus changing forever the history of its original inhabitants. In actual history, large-scale Irish emigration began in the eighteenth century when many travelled to the New World due to political and religious conflicts. By the middle of the nineteenth century, the large-scale disaster of the Irish potato-crop failure and the outbreak of widespread famine resulted in a sharp reduction of approximately one-quarter of the population, among which about one million died of starvation and disease and another million were forced to abandon their homes. That period saw Ireland's biggest wave of emigration. Since then, until the late twentieth century – in fact not long before the birth of *Riverdance* – Ireland had almost the highest emigration rate in Europe

In this new world, Ireland's traditional music and dance began to face different and unknown cultures. Perhaps it was the process of cultural integration that allowed these immigrants to find new modes of expression that incorporated a larger and more meaningful representation of the human experience. As already mentioned, the reason why *Riverdance* can be highly valued internationally is due principally to the collision and integration of Irish cultural elements with those of other cultures. The transformation brought by a new kind of 'intercultural' experience might be seen as a crucial catalyst in the *Riverdance* phenomenon. Certainly such intercultural mediation happened not by design but by historical accident. Such encounters are played out in Act Twelve, "The Harbour of the New World', in the dance sequence 'Trading Taps' that juxtaposes Irish and African American dance styles and, finally, in 'Andalusia', in which the passionate rhythm of Latin music conveys the exuberant ambience of the streets.

When placed within a Chinese context, the 'resonance' brought about by what has been, historically, a similar river culture, embraces the rushing energy of *Finnegans Wake* as well as its 'riverrun' practice of fusing myth and history through different languages, whether of words or dance. In fact, the title of the first, original 1994 Eurovision production was called 'The River'. Such an implicit connection between the two cultures allows the *Riverdance* audience better able to embrace its unique energy. In his introduction to *Riverdance*, the theatre producer Zhang Ligang remarks:

> We are originally a nation that is accustomed to using dance, rhythm and music to convey emotions, pursue love and eulogize life. *Riverdance* evokes these natural and unrestrained, casual, energetic and creative drives that have precipitated in our bones and blood. This is one of the reasons why the Chinese audience and *Riverdance* are deeply attracted and attached to each other.

In addition, every place *Riverdance* goes, its creators make clear attempts to blend in with the local music culture. During its tours in China, the *Riverdance* creative team includes such Chinese traditional musical set-pieces as 'My Motherland' and the 'Love Song in Kangding' while coordinating them with well-known Chinese symbols. When these songs occur at the climax of the performance, they almost take people's breath away.

Conclusion

As it has now become a key symbol of Irish ethnicity for China, *Riverdance* is playing a very important role in the construction of Ireland's cultural identity. It has brought Irish dance to the world while, at the same time, changing the original appearance of Irish dance. Yet, as it is both commercial and profitable, some are inclined to believe that the cultural authenticity and avowed ethnic identity of *Riverdance* are suspect.

Such questions aside, it can only be said that, while arousing the masses, *Riverdance* has also brought about a new homogeneity for Irish step dancing. In some sense, the *Riverdance* style has become global, at a distinct remove from the traditional stiff, lower-body dancing of little ringleted girls whose skirts were ornamented with Celtic symbols. But this distance is invisible to non-professionals in the audience who certainly believe that *Riverdance* represents the authentic, original Irish step dance.

Yet from the perspective of historical development, it is safe to say that culture itself is built by people from different times and diverse backgrounds. In our opinion, the success of *Riverdance* is not an accident simply because it is praiseworthy in its original artistic content or because of its highly market-oriented production and operation. In the final analysis, its success is owed to its all-embracing nature in the ways it has broken through cultural and national boundaries. In the era when a Chinese voice is badly needed and Chinese culture is being exported (by such means as the Confucius Institutes) all over the world, it seems we can learn something from its success.

Riverdance makes us think how Irish people – who at times seemed to be pouring into other parts of the world like a river – are in fact standing in the river of history and looking back to the source of their culture. They have displayed the greatness of a nation that could not be obliterated by the forces of a history that they survived with their soaring voice and with aroused and defiant steps.

Maybe it is time for China to create its own *Riverdance*?

Doing Irish Business in China

Kieran Fitzgerald

Shortly after assuming power in 2012, Premier Xi Jinping announced that 'Realizing the great renewal of the Chinese nation is the dream for the Chinese nation in modern history.' With that goal in mind, he introduced his plan to revitalize China to former international greatness – a greatness seen to have been merely interrupted in the last century due to foreign invasions and the 'setback', or 'ten years of madness', of the Cultural Revolution, which paved the way for the formation of China as we know it today. Now with a GDP of over €10 trillion in 2017, it is no surprise that the eyes of the world are on a rising China.

In terms of food (the area in which I work), China is a huge, fragmented country with a rich culinary history. It officially has eight distinct cuisines (Shandong, Sichuan, Hunan, Guangdong, Zhejiang, Jiangsu, Anhui and Fujian). But in reality there is much more diversity than that, as these designations do not include many of the fifty or more 'minority nationalities' scattered across such regions as Yunnan. Its very diversity points to an important truth: food is central to Chinese civilization – and has been, for a very long time. Perhaps an old joke might illustrate this. A Westerner and his Chinese colleague are walking in the hills above Beijing. A small brown furry creature streaks across their path. 'What is it?' the Westerner demands. 'I don't know,' the colleague shrugs. 'I was just wondering whether it was good to eat.'

'Good to eat' is important in China. But what qualities now make food in China good to eat? Because they can be advertised as 'good to eat', Irish agri-food products are enjoying significant success there today. China is in fact Ireland's third largest export market, with a value of almost €1 billion in 2017. This is more than double what it was in 2013, making agri-food Ireland's single biggest material export to China. Such rapid growth demonstrates both the positive reception and great potential of this market. To break these figures down, China is Ireland's second most important market for dairy and third overall for pork. In this country of 1.4 billion people, the size of the market often requires large volumes of goods - so the 'big players' have been the ones reaping the largest rewards until now. Although we may seem comparatively small players, Irish products such as Kerrygold butter and cheese, Avonmore milk, SuperValu own-brand products and the like are readily available in traditional Chinese supermarkets from Shanghai to Chengdu as well as online. Guinness, Jameson and Baileys are other Irish brands common in supermarkets and bars throughout the country. As of 2018 Irish beef is now also available on China's two largest online retail outlets, Tmall and JD.com. How has this happened?

A new growth in consumerism follows China's 'burgeoning middle class'. Since the early 1980s China's urban middle class — now with significant and growing spending power — has gone from near zero to 430 million people today. This group is expected to reach 1 billion people by 2030, or 70 per cent of projected population. As these people become even more affluent, they are demanding more protein, whether through dairy, meat, or seafood products. Direct air routes from Ireland (the first two of which commenced operation in June 2018) help to get such produce to market quicker. These air routes are more relevant for short-shelf-life products such as live seafood, a popular import from Ireland — ensuring they also are good to eat.

'Good to Eat'

What is 'good to eat', however, has changed over the last twenty-five years, as the Chinese economy has recorded consistent and remarkable growth. A new official focus on growing urbanization has led to consumers' increasing wages and busier lifestyles along with rising demand for new products, in food as elsewhere. So far, total food consumption was forecast to grow on average by 9.3 per cent per annum to reach €939 billion by 2018 or €660 per capita. As consumers become more affluent, they are developing a taste for premium products, including imported food. In fact, the number of foreign food stores in large cities such as Beijing and Shanghai is growing – and they are increasingly patronized by affluent Chinese customers as well as gastronomically nostalgic expatriates.

But what do the Chinese regard as good food? As Bord Bia (the Irish Food Board) has learned that, in order to access the Chinese market, the highest food safety standards are required. China is not known for its own food safety, but with the vast scale of this fragmented industry, quality control is admittedly hard to manage. Much easier to control are China's national borders, with Chinese customs regulations among the strictest in the world. Doing business with China is facilitated by its government mapping out its projected economic development in five-year segments. The current Five Year Plan (2016–20) is the thirteenth since Chairman Mao Zedong initiated the first one in 1953. Significantly, food security has featured in the past five consecutive Five-Year Plans.

On the Irish side, Bord Bia is currently running a three-year (2017–19) €3.75 million project, co-financed by the EU, in China, Hong Kong and Japan promoting the food safety, sustainability and traceability attributes of European beef and lamb, using Ireland as the model of best practice. Luckily, the EU enjoys a reputation for high food safety and quality standards. Ireland, a tiny country on the edge of Europe that many tens (possibly hundreds) of millions of people in China have never heard of, greatly benefits from this association with the EU's high standards.

Overview: Agri-food Exports

It is a little-known fact that Ireland produces *five times* more food than it consumes. We have been a food-producing and exporting island for centuries. Even during the Great Famine – when British colonial administrators diverted much-needed food to England – these exports continued even as people at home literally starved to death.

Over the centuries, the export network we in Ireland have developed means that it can find markets for parts of the animal that may not be desired at home. Take Irish pork, for example. As is well known, China is the largest pig-meat producer and consumer in the world – and demand for imports continues to rise. In this context, Irish pig meat has enjoyed significant success, with Ireland exporting over €100 million worth to China in 2017. Such is the demand that Ireland can include in its exports items such as pig offal, heads, or trotters, which have in recent generations become unpopular in Ireland – just as they are enjoying greater popularity elsewhere.

Today the main Irish food exports to China are dairy, meat and seafood. However, with exports of almost €760 million (including Hong Kong) in 2017, dairy is leading the pack by a long way (both in volume and value), infant milk formula being the main driver in this success. The price paid for infant milk formula is much higher in China than in most other countries. The premium Illuma (Wyeth) and Green Love (Beingmate) brands, well known by young mothers all over the country, strongly promote their Irish infant milk formula (note that, although the product is Irish, the brands belong to non-Irish companies, much like Guinness, Jameson and Baileys). As Ireland looks to increase dairy exports, this is good news for the eighteen thousand Irish dairy farmers. Since the lifting of EU milk quotas in 2016, much of the additional capacity went to Asia. And in Asia, China is the world's biggest importer of many agri-food products, including dairy.

An unlikely ally for Irish dairy has been China's controversial one-child policy, in force for over three decades until October 2015. Thirty-five years of only children has led to generations of 'little emperors', who sit at the top of the household hierarchy. The focus of all of their parents' attention and ambition, they may also be the parents' only pension policy. Many of these children are also often the only grandchildren – which can lead to their being the object of lavished resources from up to six doting adults. Along with this comes intense pressure to succeed. To enable the precious child to always do his best, the parents must supply the right food – which starts with the right milk formula and healthy protein to supplement breastfeeding. After all, the Chinese mantra – a central tenet of their cuisine – is that 'food is medicine'.

But 'good food' is often seen as scarce in China. A history of domestic food-safety scandals means that for China's middle class their own and their children's health has been a matter of intense and ongoing concern. In the most infamous of Chinese food scandals, in 2008 domestic infant milk formula was found to contain melamine, a chemical used in the production of plastics, cement and fertilizers. Six babies died and 300,000 fell ill as a result. The resulting decline in trust in domestic products coincided with a rapid increase in Chinese consumers' purchasing power along with new access to imported products for which the Chinese consumer is ready to pay a premium price. Since then Irish infant milk formula has successfully earned its place in a premium market segment. In 2017 Ireland was the second largest supplier of premium milk powder in China.

Under these circumstances, demand for dairy is expected to continue to increase. To attempt to describe the scale of this market: if China's dairy consumption were to increase from 10 kilograms per person per year to Japanese levels of 60 kilograms per person per year, China would require an additional 70 million tons of dairy, dwarfing Ireland's total dairy production. While other dairy products such as yoghurt, cheese and butter are also being well received, a significant challenge is how to convince people to purchase items not usually a traditional part of their diet.

Among these non-traditional foods is beef. Historically, in China beef has not been a food 'good to eat'. While consumption of beef in China is low, as with any other developing country, as people have higher incomes, beef consumption rises. China banned the import of beef from the EU after the well-documented BSE [*Bovine Spongiform Encephalopathy*, commonly known as 'mad cow disease'] outbreak in Europe in the early 2000s. Following this crisis, Ireland was the first major European beef-exporting country to regain access to the Chinese market (Hungary also gained access in 2014 but does not export significant quantities), with the first shipment of Irish beef landing on Chinese shores in July 2018. This achievement was not as simple as it looks: from getting approval to actually shipping a product, there are seven steps to go through. Currently Ireland has access to the Chinese market for frozen, boneless beef from animals under thirty months old (no offal is currently permitted).

Although beef has not traditionally been a major part of the Chinese diet, demand there is increasing – whereas, ironically, it is decreasing for certain kinds of beef elsewhere. As in the case of pork, many beef cuts, such as tongue, shank and brisket are no longer popular in Western markets – no longer regarded as convenient to cook or 'good to eat'. Yet there is still a place for these products in modern Chinese cuisine, with the result that Irish beef now finds a highly compatible as well as lucrative market.

So in 2018, Irish beef has been the big story for the Irish export market. It is worth noting, however, that annual consumption of beef in China is still under 4 kilograms per person per year, compared to 6.7 kilograms in Japan and almost 11 kilograms in the EU. If Chinese consumption of beef rises by even 1 kilogram per person per year, China would need to import 1.2 million additional tonnes of beef to meet this demand. To put this in context, total Irish beef exports are roughly 535,000 tonnes of beef per year. Irish supply continues to increase just as demand in traditional European markets is slowing, making China a logical alternative. The Department of Agriculture and the Marine, and the Department of Foreign Affairs and Trade along with Bord Bia now need to cooperate robustly in pursuing expansion of our beef access if they wish to capitalize on the significant opportunity that China currently represents.

In tandem with the beef market, the seafood market has just had another record year in China. With sales of over €38 million, such products as brown crab, whelk, razor clams and oysters have proved to be the most popular items here. Again – with the exception of oysters – these are all products that are not so common in Irish supermarkets or on menus but are considered premium in China – and therefore available to export abroad.

Risks: the Chinese Market

With such statistics, one might think that Ireland's food-marketing future in China is rosy, to say the least. In fact, this is far from the case. The Chinese market poses its own significant challenges; anyone doing business, or aspiring to do business, there needs to be keenly aware of these.

For instance: 'good to eat' is now a highly scrutinized term. Within the Chinese context, any kind of food safety scare would be disastrous.

The Chinese government has become very sensitive to any issues surrounding food safety; it will not hesitate to block imports immediately if there is even the suspicion of a problem. Particularly regarding infant milk formula, the markets are hypersensitive; understandably so, given the recent trauma associated with this product. In fact, the Chinese government's State Administration of Market Regulation now contains a specialized infant milk formula recipe division (this used to be part of the Food and Drug Administration which no longer exists since the recent government reshuffle). By such means, the government is also attempting to rebuild trust in domestic infant milk formula producers, as low consumer confidence has led to imported products occupying 60 per cent of the market (a figure that is continuing to grow). In response, the Chinese government is seeking fewer but larger domestic producers. Currently approximately eighty domestic factories produce over three thousand brands. Reducing the number of producers would of course make them easier to regulate, thus ensuring their quality. As a consequence, foreign producers are restricted on the amounts of brands they can produce for the Chinese market.

Marketing Irish beef also brings its own problems. Ireland is attempting to promote a product that is traditionally not a popular part of consumers' diet (outside of communities such as the Tibetans and Mongolians who rear their own beef, usually in the form of yak). Despite the variety of Chinese cuisines, meat is usually prepared in chunks or thin slices then cooked in woks or stewing pots. Few consumers own ovens – although they are becoming more popular with everyone's target market, the burgeoning middle class. Also Irish beef tends to be more expensive than that exported by many of our competitors; therefore it is essential to communicate to consumers how to use this premium product to realize its value. Another issue, our greatest natural advantage and Ireland's major selling point: we have a temperate climate, a comparatively pristine environment with lots of rain and fertile soil that results in lush green grass that allows cattle to graze outside more often than in practically any other country in the world. As close to an organic system as you can get, perhaps. The result is our beautiful grass-fed beef: clearly 'good to eat'. Yet Chinese consumers, not educated in the original food cycle of cows, prefer grain-fed over grass-fed beef – perhaps one of the markers of their conceptual distance from what we in the West regard as 'natural'.

So Irish exporters and Bord Bia have their work cut out for them. The numerous consumer research projects that we administer take up a lot of resources, but much research is necessary to launch and run a successful advertising campaign. The online landscape in China is completely different than in Europe – or indeed most markets. Social media platforms like Wechat and Weibo are king. They are the most trusted sources of information on many topics including food safety and quality. Google, Facebook, Twitter, YouTube and Instagram are all blocked. Much of the country has gone almost cashless in the last three years or so. In Shanghai there are stores that no longer accept cash or card payments – mobile payments only. To say that the local culture is different is an obvious understatement. Business and family relationships are also quite different to what we are used to – numerous books have been written on the subject. And then there is the issue of the language. China is a market where image is all important; in this area, Irish products already start off a step or two behind more prestigious national brands such as those coming from France, the US, or Australia. While the infant milk formula industry has managed to carve out a premium image, other markets still have to learn from this success if they are to follow suit.

Economics

As a small country with the population of a medium-sized Chinese city, Ireland tends to punch above its weight in many areas – in the arts (Wilde, Yeats, Joyce, Shaw, U2 and *Riverdance* are already well known in China), in sport, in inward investment as well as agri-food production and its exports. As a major supplier of agricultural products to Great Britain for centuries, Ireland already has a developed and export-oriented agri-food industry, now with markets worldwide. As of 2017, we export products to over 180 countries across the globe. The value of these exports in 2017 was over €12 billion – making the agri-food business Ireland's largest indigenous industry.

The year 2017 marked the eighth successive year of growth in agri-food exports. Much of the growth in exports is in emerging international markets outside of our traditionally strongest, established customers – the European Union and UK. Of these, dairy accounted for over 30 per cent of all agri-food exports and beef almost 20 per cent. The sector itself accounts for around 167,500 jobs, the majority of which are in rural Ireland, important for delivering much needed rural employment. In terms of balances of international payments, every €100 of exports from the sector generates €52 in net foreign earnings, in contrast to only €19 in net foreign earnings from other sectors.

Risks: the Irish Market

Again, any food scare would clearly have a substantial impact on the Irish economy. The BSE crisis of the early 2000s – a result of contaminated feed that has since been banned in Ireland – is still fresh in the minds of everyone in the industry. It cost the Irish economy over €1 billion.

Meanwhile, stricter food safety controls through the Irish supply chain – from farm to processor to retailer – greatly reduce the risk of another such crisis. We cannot afford to be complacent. Bord Bia is already designing a number of crisis management plans to be ready to react should another catastrophe in the Irish agri-food industry emerge. There is another layer of protection too, as the EU can boast some of the world's highest food safety controls. Yet another risk arises from the Chinese government's policy of seeking to reduce the demand for imported as against domestic products, especially in the domestic infant milk formula industry. For the future, we cannot know what kind of protectionism could be implemented in the name of a new nationalism. While demand for imported products is expected to continue to increase, it is important for government agencies and exporters to have crisis management and contingency plans in place. In this context, 'fail to prepare' may indeed mean 'prepare to fail'.

Finally, Brexit clearly poses a major threat to the Irish agri-food industry. Over 50 per cent of Irish beef and 60 per cent of cheddar exports now go to the UK. We have been exporting to the UK for centuries; thus the unknown threat that Brexit represents is understandably worrying. As markets hate uncertainty, we are trying to offset Ireland's traditional reliance on UK exports by working even harder to develop Chinese and other Asian markets. Expanding exports to emerging markets has never been more important. For instance, China is becoming an increasingly attractive market for cheese, which is at the moment the most exposed to any downturn in its UK business. At the time of writing, with the outcome of Brexit negotiations still as clear as mud, a potential crisis is looming for the agri-food industry.

Of course, we in Ireland all hope that the worst-case scenario Brexit will not materialize or that the 'new normal' will become manageable. But such a scenario highlights the importance of spreading risk over multiple markets while being prepared for any emergency. Within the next few years China is set to become the first billion-euro market for Irish agri-food exports. An acknowledgement of the growing importance of China as an export market is reflected in the size of Bord Bia's office in Shanghai: its second biggest international office after that in the USA. Such an increased access to the market will help to reduce the pain of a potential 'Hard Brexit', but it certainly could not absorb the full damage overnight.

Even now, the threat of Brexit teaches us all a lesson about *not* putting all of our eggs in the China, or any other, basket. Still, other countries such as Australia and New Zealand are now far more dependent on China than Ireland. We have learned, and will probably have to learn again, the hard lesson that it is always important to diversify.

The Strength of Ireland's Green Image

Ireland has long enjoyed, as well as used, its green credentials to promote food and tourism. Bord Bia in particular invokes Ireland's comparatively clean environment as being ideal for producing food. But Ireland's image of a land of rolling hills, of patchwork green fields with cows grazing in lush grass pastures, no longer suffices as a selling point. New Zealand, Australia, Canada, Germany are all pushing the same message – and, more importantly, are also perceived to be 'clean' by Chinese consumers. So it is no longer enough to say you are green and clean: you must be able to prove it. Hence Bord Bia's Origin Green programme, which proclaims Ireland as the only country in the world with a national-level sustainability programme for the whole food industry. We point out that we have been blessed with natural advantages. Also Ireland never went through an industrial revolution involving a heavy manufacturing industry that resulted (as in the UK) in historically massive pollution of air, soil and water. At a time when most countries in Europe were going through their industrial revolutions, Ireland remained backward, the site of ongoing rebellions and famines. Now (ironically) this failure to develop can be seen as a huge advantage.

But this advantage is also under challenge. As the global population is increasing and natural resources decreasing, the food industry uses a lot of resources that are becoming increasingly scarce. The global challenge for the food industry is how to produce more with less. With the escalating threats of climate change (in particular to water resources), it is ever more important that Ireland can demonstrate its environmental credentials.

Thus in 2012 Bord Bia launched the Origin Green programme with the goal of having every food-producing business in Ireland signed up to a national sustainability charter. To date there are over 600 registered companies carrying out audits of over 212,000 carbon footprints on farms to determine the total impact of all the greenhouse gases that contribute to global warming. What this means in practice is that Bord Bia assesses every farm in Ireland at least once every eighteen months for harmful environmental emissions. Currently no other country is measuring the carbon footprint of its farms on a national scale. On top of this, quality assurance programmes, in place for over twenty years in Ireland, are being constantly improved and updated. Produce from these quality assured farms generally earns a premium price from processors, further illustrating Ireland's national and cohesive commitment to sustainability. Implementing such controls also saves water, reduces waste, decreases energy use and, by cutting food producers' costs, improves their profits. The overall intention is that Ireland will become the most carbon-efficient food producer in Europe. Already our dairy and beef herds can boast one of the lowest carbon footprints in Europe.

Being able so clearly and quantifiably to demonstrate the sustainability efforts of Ireland's food industry sends a powerful message, making Origin Green an effective marketing tool for the agri-food industry. However, recent reports that Ireland is set to miss out badly on 2020 (and possibly 2030 and 2050) climate-change targets has the potential to damage the green image Ireland has been building over the years. Negative press about a first-world country that cannot keep its climate-change commitments risks being trotted out as an example. For instance, how can the West put pressure on China to improve its environmental performance if Ireland is doing so poorly? What if Ireland manages to lose its main selling point? Worse, what if we were seen to be simply environmental frauds? It is yet to be seen how this situation will develop over the next decade. One can only hope that Ireland's performance stays on track. But, right now, any negative international news would not be conducive to promoting Ireland's marketing efforts.

Assuming, however, that Ireland retains its green, sustainable image, thus ensuring that Origin Green remains a credible marketing tool, the next question is: who cares? Literally: who cares that Ireland is the only country in the world with a national-level sustainability programme? Is 'good food' on this level only a kind of moral good? In fact, a lot of enlightened people do care, as they should. But do the Chinese middle-class consumers, who will soon represent the majority of that nation's population, know enough about these issues to care about them? Ultimately, will their concern for food quality convert into increased sales of Irish food and drink in China? My own experience working in one of China's great nature reserves may offer some perspective on these questions.

Environmental Sustainability: Chinese Middle-Class Attitudes

In considering China's relationship to the environment, it is important to recall that a word for 'nature' did not even exist in Mandarin until imported from Japan just over a hundred years ago. When the word did begin to be used, it was with an entirely different resonance than in the West. Whereas for most Westerners 'nature' is considered to be divinely created, for the Chinese the world is designated as *ziran*, meaning self-generated or 'so-of-itself'. Although it is defined as having more or less harmonious interrelations as the 'natural' conditions of things, *ziran* invokes no higher ordering principle or agency: in other words, 'nature' is not divine nor does it speak of the divine. It is thus present to be used, enjoyed – and exploited – without the residual reverence attached to it by those enculturated in Western ways of thinking. It is for this reason among others (such as poverty) that ecology is only now becoming a conscious issue among China's more educated classes.

Having spent over five years working in Jiuzhaigou National Park, China's premier nature reserve, I experienced the Chinese middle-class relationship with nature first hand and on a daily basis. Continuous observation over this time gave me a useful insight into actual Chinese attitudes towards the environment. Jiuzhaigou National Park is China's foremost natural tourism destination. It is a place that most Chinese people aspire to visit once in their lives. It ranks on a similar level as the Forbidden City and the Great Wall on the bucket list of a billion people. Famed for its specular scenery, lakes and waterfalls, Jiuzhaigou is often featured on lists of China's best eco-destinations by reputable travel publications. It has provided the backdrop for some of China's most successful international blockbuster movies, such as *Crouching Tiger, Hidden Dragon* and *Hero*. Its ethereal beauty makes it a kind of fairy land that Chinese people are rightly proud of.

Although Jiuzhaigou has been designated a UNESCO World Heritage Site since 1993, it was opened as an official eco-tourism programme only sixteen years later. Its first eco-accommodation, A Bu Lu Zi Eco Lodge, opened in 2015. Those Chinese tourists that choose to stay in the remote valley where the park is located have an interest in eco-tourism and are largely well-educated, affluent tourists who really enjoy the experience alongside their international counterparts. Domestic visitors that do not fit into this category generally regret choosing the Eco Lodges, as do their hosts. The accommodation is simpler, nearer to the original homes of the community which lives in the valley. Accordingly, the vast majority of Jiuzhaigou's tourists prefer the modern luxuries of the large hotels located in a strip development around the park entrance.

Some context is needed here. In Jiuzhaigou, the local Tibetan community have for centuries lived largely in harmony with nature. Unlike their Chinese visitors, they regard the natural world with reverence, as their *Bon* spiritual beliefs stipulate that they should respect everything with a soul: that includes not only living creatures but also the sky, clouds, mountains, water and earth. Unfortunately, the introduction of plastics, glass and other man-made packaging into this environment has come without education on how to dispose of it. Ignorance has led to it being disposed of as litter or burned in fires.

It is true that environmental values and attitudes in developing countries are usually luxuries that come after making money. Even for the local community – composed of people who have an ancestral and religious tie to the land – a lack of education and a desire for economic development would result in the environment being pushed further down the list of priorities. If a subsistence farmer is told he can eradicate a persistent pest by spraying a product once or twice a year – and that by doing so, he can make his life easier and make more money – the likelihood is he will go ahead and use the product. Traditional systems – such as farming methods, fertilizing, recycling, waste disposal and even hunting of wild animals for consumption – are usually sustainable. It is the introduction of outside products and methods along with increasing numbers of mouths to feed that makes these time-honoured methods unsustainable. However environmentally friendly local Tibetan farmers would like to be, they usually have limited or no awareness of the wider impact of their actions. By way of contrast, in Ireland we have the necessary policies in place to create a national-level sustainability programme. In general, society does adhere to rules; but these rules were not made overnight: they have taken decades (and membership in the European Union) to evolve. Indeed, it might have been EU membership that ultimately saved Irish farming from exactly these dangers.

In general, eco-tourism is defined as tourism to natural areas that is environmentally friendly as well as beneficial to local communities, their culture and their economy. However, many eco-tourism experiences in China are limited to the single idea of tourism to natural areas. Thus for the Chinese visiting Jiuzhaigou (as with other natural tourist destinations in China) the experience can be more akin to their visiting a theme park. Activities for the vast majority of tourists include getting on a bus, getting off for a quick photo of themselves and their party at each site, eating food that they are used to at home, drinking and (finally) getting locals to sing and dance for them. Local communities will often degrade their own cultures to entertain these lucrative groups who can book out their property or service for the whole season.

In 2007, the vast majority of guests came to Jiuzhaigou by travel-agent tour. The park shut down for most of 2008 after the Sichuan Earthquake in which almost a hundred thousand people perished or were declared missing. Tourism slowly started coming back in 2009. In the short time between May 2008 and May 2010 the speed of economic development in China had pulled millions of people into the middle class and millions of families, for the first time, could afford their own car. The age of road trips was born! On the newly upgraded roads up the Min Jiang valley from Chengdu and her numerous satellite cities, and up the highways across the Tibetan Plateau to the North, packed cars with registration plates from all over China descended on Jiuzhaigou. The few green spaces on the valley floor were concreted over to make car parks. Tourism numbers increased from about 2.5 million in 2007 to twice that in 2015.

Observing the actions of tourists as well as staff at Jiuzhaigou – or at other natural tourist destinations in China – would suggest that a lot of the talk of environmental protection is not much more than that: just talk. Their lack of adequate response stems from a lack of environmental education. As was once the case in Ireland and most developed countries, the first generation that could afford tourism was not made up of environmental angels. The more educated and affluent tourists from big cities to Jiuzhaigou are generally more environmentally aware: they act accordingly. They are less likely to be seen climbing trees, smoking, dropping litter, or even relieving themselves in the national park than their counterparts from other segments of Chinese society.

It is a good sign that there is an increasing demand for this kind of experience from the upper middle class, but it has its price. Accommodation in Jiuzhaigou once consisted of mostly non-local owned hotels and guest houses that operated during seven months of the year with non-local staff: this has had only limited benefit to the local economy. In recent years a number of domestically owned, internationally branded high-end chain hotels have moved in, looking to capitalize on wealthy tourists' desire for an eco-experience. In one particular valley that was largely untouched until a few years ago – home to three local villages with a population of about a thousand – four massive hotel projects have moved in. They have been constructed with taste, but the scale is certainly not in harmony with the surroundings, having over a thousand rooms in total.

One cannot blame these hotels for wanting to capitalize on this affluent market; after all they were granted planning permission, so why should they not build there? However, these hotels will send the majority of their tourists into the valley in which they are located, having a negative impact on this, until now largely untouched, local eco-system. I hope I am wrong about the impact these visitors will have and what environmental protection measures the hotels might install; but history has taught me to be sceptical of optimistic outcomes. Jiuzhaigou and the neighbouring Huanglong National Parks account for over 30 per cent of the larger prefecture's revenue. This revenue has been built on a mass tourism model. Under these circumstances it is clear that a model of low number, low-impact tourism is not about to be implemented in China any time soon.

This is a lesson I had to learn the hard way. Shortly after arriving in Jiuzhaigou in 2007 as a sustainable development consultant, I shared my opinion on the amount of energy waste in the national park administration. It was suggested that I write a report on my observations. Although the report was well received, not one of my recommendations was acted upon. For example, the lack of adequate refuse services leads to some business owners emptying their bins into the river at night. More significantly, waste water is making its way into the formerly pristine main water course. Although conditions are improving, it has taken a long time. This particular experience goes some way to highlight the ways in which actual sustainability within the environment, both from a governmental and general population point of view, is often not much more than a facade.

Not surprisingly, then, in China eco-tourism and sustainability are often victims of significant 'green-washing': a form of spin in which green PR or green marketing is deceptively used to promote the perception that an organization's project, aims or policies are environmentally friendly. The majority of tourism in Jiuzhaigou is merely mass tourism to a natural site, quite the opposite of true eco-tourism. This may be the same for the food industry. In order to be concerned about sustainability in this area, one needs to focus on consumers who are concerned with sustainability in their everyday lives, not just when making purchases or travel decisions. As Bord Bia research has suggested, consumers that consider the sustainability of a potential purchase as its most important selling point are the well-educated and affluent 'super super premium' segment (significantly more likely customers than the merely 'super premium' for whom food safety is the major priority). People in large cities with a good income and a good education are the ones that seem to be the most 'eco-friendly'. As in much of the world, sustainability appears to be a luxury, one desired, or at least first adopted, more by upper classes or the highly educated rather than the masses.

It is to the majority of these more environmentally alert consumers that Ireland's joint focus on food safety and sustainability should appeal. Here Ireland is in a strong position, as it can clearly prove our commitment to sustainability in food production. The positive aspect for Ireland is that the sheer scale of the Chinese market means that the numbers of the 'super super premium' educated consumers will easily eclipse the total of those in the UK market.

Political Sustainability: Irish Diplomatic and Agency Efforts

Regardless of consumer motivations for making particular food or drink purchases, getting these products into the market is the first and most important step. The success Ireland has enjoyed to date could not have been achieved without close cooperation with the Chinese government. Ireland regaining beef access was a result of many years of persistent, high-level political engagement from a number of Irish government departments and agencies.

Diplomatic relations are more important in some countries than others; China is one where they are crucial. For many years, Irish diplomatic efforts on the ground have been conducted by the coordinated efforts of the Department of Foreign Affairs; the Department of Agriculture, Food and the Marine; Bord Bia; Enterprise Ireland and Tourism Ireland. All have been instrumental in regaining beef access, though it took Ireland eighteen years. The access agreement had to go through a three-year, seven-stage process to get final permission to export. In its most recent diplomatic efforts, Ireland also succeeded in securing direct flights from Beijing and Hong Kong to Dublin beginning in June 2018, thus supporting the large export market in perishable products, such as Irish seafood.

These developments highlight the importance of high-level diplomatic relations and governmental visits between both countries. As part of the 2025 Global Ireland plan, Ireland is to double its representative presence overseas over the next seven years; this includes China, where a new consulate has already been opened in Hong Kong. But developing and nurturing diplomatic relations is a long-term process. Just as access has been granted, so can it also be revoked or barriers increased. That Ireland is the first major European beef exporter to be granted such access since the BSE crisis in 2001 is testimony to not only the strength of our industry but also the evolving political relationship between Ireland and China.

At their most effective, these are based on personal diplomacy coupled with actual site visits. Thus, over the course of its three-year (2017–20) EU beef and lamb campaign, Bord Bia – in partnership with the Department of Agriculture, Food and the Marine – will bring sixty Chinese government officials to Ireland to highlight our excellent food safety standards. The original visit to Ireland in 2012 of then vice-president Xi Jinping – in particular his stop-off at a dairy farm in Clare – generated a great deal of good will, several trade agreements and a chance to see the Irish countryside for himself. Such personal government-to-government relationships are essential to attaining, expanding and building on our developing ties with China. Bringing Chinese influencers to Ireland often goes a long way. But, of course, a key political risk when dealing with China is its sensitivity to criticism. China's track record on human rights, its censorship, its specific environment issues, as well as those surrounding sovereignty and territorial claims have been sources of debate in the West for decades. The regrettable reality is that one comment that is deemed 'anti-China' by a foreign government official can stop trade or travel in a heartbeat. As eager as Ireland is to continue to advance its business, diplomatic and political ties with China, its representatives must always be aware of the potential risks involved.

Importance of Coordinated Promotions and Efforts

As mentioned previously, the majority of China's 1.4 billion citizens have never heard of Ireland. Those Irish government agencies already present in the market are operating on restricted budgets. In order to ensure that the sum of marketing efforts is greater than the sum of individual marketing budgets, efforts must be coordinated by a 'Team Ireland' mentality to boost awareness of Ireland and its image. This could include cross-marketing, joint events, new means of sharing outcomes – among many other options. Using one marketing agency for all of 'Team Ireland' could go a long way to realizing these goals.

Such cooperation might also present new opportunities within the Irish food industry as a whole. Ireland is a small country that has limited capacity compared to some competitors. Large importers can pressure smaller exporters on price and conditions. Pressure from importers can increase competition between exporters and drive prices down, which can result in a race to the bottom, benefiting only the Chinese importers. In 2012, Bord Bia and Bord Iascaigh Mhara (the Fisheries Board), worked with four Irish seafood companies to form one company for the Chinese market. This is an excellent example of 'coopetition' where these traditional competitors are now partners for the Chinese market alone. This initiative increases their scale and bargaining power in China. Now that they have pooled resources to recruit a full-time Chinese representative to coordinate the Chinese market, they can boast of a maximally efficient approach – and one that might be profitably copied in other instances.

Cultural Sustainability: *Guanxi*

Anybody reading this essay will most likely have enough prior interest in China to be familiar with the term *guanxi*. Essentially, it means relationships, but as with most Chinese concepts, the meaning goes a lot deeper than its translation implies. *Guanxi* is everything in China – without *guanxi* nothing gets done and pretty much everything is done through it. One simply cannot write about doing business in China without mentioning it, as *guanxi* – in terms of ongoing reciprocal relationships built on mutual trust – is at the very heart of doing business itself. In practical terms, presidential and prime ministerial visits to China help build *guanxi*. While the last visits by an Irish president and prime minister were in 2012 and 2014 respectively, one can expect some high-level visits to be planned for 2019, the anniversary of forty years of diplomatic relations between the two countries (as celebrated, for example, by the publication of this book).

For Irish companies doing business in China today, *guanxi* is at a different level compared to where it was five or ten years ago. The goalposts have been moved. The basic protocols of the two-handed business-card exchange, the significance of the post-meeting meal, of its seating arrangement and – even more importantly – the drinking at that meal are still as crucial as ever. Contracts are still not worth the paper they are printed on; all and everything weighs on the quality of one's personal relationship with the proposed business partner. Doing and saying the right things at dinner will help, but forging a personal relationship in their mother tongue opens up much more understanding, rapport and opportunity. (Maybe China is not so different from the West after all!) It is important for companies and government agencies to maintain these relationships by meeting 'socially' – not only when you have an event or need something done – as Chinese people really prize these relationships as something of great value.

Cultural sustainability also depends on how you speak. Using Communist Party language is a great way to strike the right chords in Chinese consumers' minds. But the most effective tactic is to speak in your host's own tongue. In terms of learning another language, Chinese is an ancient, complex and deep language. Communicating through broken English or by means of translators has many limitations. Speaking through a translator hired from a Chinese company may also have the added complexity of a hierarchy gap between the translator and your contact. That can have a significant impact on how your message gets delivered. And – much more so than in English – it is *how* you say something, rather than *what* you say, that is most important. It is true that working at diplomatic level or within a multinational company one may get away with not speaking Chinese, although it is hugely appreciated and therefore beneficial if you do.

In dealing with food importers, distributors and customers around the country, however, the Chinese language is essential. When I first arrived in China eleven years ago, the number of foreigners speaking Chinese was quite low; the number of Irish people with fluent Chinese even less. However, in 2018 when Bord Bia was interviewing for a Chinese-speaking role, there were Chinese-speaking Irish applicants who were not even called to interview, so intense was the competition. Moreover, the standard of those that were interviewed was very impressive. This is the result of the first generation of Irish graduates emerging from the increasing number of Chinese-focused third-level courses in Ireland now with a few years of work experience under their belts. While hiring Chinese staff is and will remain essential, these are to be the employees and representatives of Ireland in China for the future.

Employing such Irish Chinese-speaking staff is thus now both achievable and necessary to keep up with our international competitors, many of whom have had Chinese-language programmes in place for a lot longer than Ireland. For all Irish companies, this would be an important step in building *guanxi*. But it is also important for the bigger picture of Ireland doing business in China. It may require taking a gamble at times, but we need to reward these graduates with career opportunities to repay their considerable investment in learning the language and also, if possible, learning about the local culture. For in China, understanding the local culture is often more important than understanding the company culture. Luckily, there are excellent graduate programmes in place in Irish companies and government agencies that give graduates a practical start in doing Irish business in China. These represent a very valuable resource that needs be taken advantage of to continue to compete in today's China, as such young Irish Chinese-speaking professionals are much in demand ('gold dust' as described by one administrator of a higher degree in Chinese Studies).

While all of this is going on in China, we in Ireland need to be 'China-ready'. This is the term being used by Fáilte Ireland (the Irish

Tourism Development Authority) to ensure Irish tourism businesses are ready to host Chinese visitors. We need to be China-ready in the public and private sectors, both in Ireland and in China. Bord Bia has increased its market presence in China over the past two years. Irish universities are also, on many fronts, preparing students to be China-ready. The challenge is now, on the occasion of forty years of diplomatic relations between China and Ireland, to engage the wider public in appreciating what has become perhaps the most adventurous – and profitable – enterprise in the history of Ireland's relationship with China. Interpreted broadly, that enterprise is much larger than the Irish agri-food industry: it is nothing less than transforming Irish and Chinese attitudes towards each other and our shared environment through the starting point of our most pragmatic interests and interactions.

Contributors

Assumpta Broomfield is a graduate of the National Botanic Gardens in Glasnevin, Dublin, and has designed many gardens in Ireland. She gives talks on various aspects of garden and plant history throughout Ireland. In 2002 she was part of a committee of the Irish Garden Plant Society that brought an exhibit entitled *Augustine Henry – An Irish Plant Collector in China* to the Chelsea Flower Show, where it received widespread interest and was awarded a Silver Gilt Medal. She was also a member of three botanical expeditions to China – in 2002, 2004 and 2005 – which followed the footsteps of Augustine Henry during his Chinese plant-collecting career.

    Chen Li is Professor of Irish Literature and Vice Director of the Irish Studies Centre in Beijing Foreign Studies University, China. In 2017–18 she was a visiting Fulbright scholar at Boston College, USA. She is the author of *Rose upon the Rood of Time: Twentieth-Century Irish Big-House Novel* (2009) and *Self-Fashioning in the Irish Literary Revival* (2016), both written in Chinese. Currently she is working on the representations of the Irish diaspora in contemporary literary works.

    Dai Congrong is a Professor of Comparative Literature and World Literature in the Faculty of Chinese Language and Literature, Fudan University, Shanghai, China, where she also holds the post of Director at the Centre for Literary Translation and Studies. She is now serving as the Chinese co-director at the Confucius Institute for Scotland, located at the University of Edinburgh. She is also a board member of the *James Joyce Quarterly*. She has published four books in Chinese, mainly on English literature, and translated six books from English, one of which is James Joyce's *Finnegans Wake* (Book One).

Luke Drury is an Emeritus Professor in the Dublin Institute for Advanced Studies and former Head of the Astronomy and Astrophysics Section of the School of Cosmic Physics who remembers Tao Kiang well and with deep affection. **Anna-Sophia Kiang** is Tao's daughter and mother to two of his grandchildren. She is a Research Fellow in genetics in Trinity College Dublin.

Kieran Fitzgerald swapped a stable career in financial services with Merrill Lynch for the edge of the Himalayan Plateau in Jiuzhaigou National Park, China's premier national park, in 2007. An initial two-year contract turned into over five years working for the Chinese government on sustainable tourism development, eco-tourism, international marketing and community projects. During the subsequent four years working in Ireland, most recently for Fáilte Ireland, Kieran continued to work closely on sustainable tourism projects with the Tibetan community in Jiuzhaigou. In 2017 he returned to Shanghai to manage Bord Bia's €3.75 million European beef and lamb promotional campaign, co-funded by the European Union and Bord Bia.

Joseph Grange was Professor Emeritus of Philosophy at the University of Southern Maine and author of several books in philosophy, including *Soul: A Cosmology*; *Nature: An Environmental Cosmology*; *City: An Urban Cosmology*; and *John Dewey, Confucius, and Global Philosophy*, all published with State University of New York Press. **Jim Behuniak** is Associate Professor and Chair of the Philosophy Department at Colby College and author of several articles in areas of Asian and comparative philosophy, including the books *Mencius on Becoming Human* and *Appreciating the Chinese Difference: Engaging Roger T. Ames on Methods, Issues, and Roles*, which he edited. Both volumes are published with State University of New York Press. Jim has edited the original essay to make it more accessible to the non-professional reader as a tribute to his late professor and mentor, Joseph Grange.

Guo Ruxin and **Hongchi Liu** are both graduate students in the Department of Musicology at Shanghai Conservatory of Music, studying for their Master's degrees in the anthropology of music. Their supervisor, Professor Xiao Mei, does research on ritual music, Chinese ethnic music, music management, performance and voice; she is also the current Chairperson of the Chinese Society for Ethnomusicology.

Lu Zhouxiang received both of his Bachelor and Master degrees in Education from universities in China and obtained his PhD at the National University of Ireland, Cork (UCC). He worked in UCC School of Asian Studies and its Irish Institute of Chinese Studies before joining Maynooth University School of Modern Languages, Literatures and Cultures in 2011 as the Subject Leader of Chinese Studies. His main research interests are Chinese history, nationalism and globalism, and comparative studies between the West and China in the field of sport. **Weiyi Wu** obtained her MA in literary theory from Renmin University in China. A PhD candidate in the School of Asian Studies in UCC, her research interests include philosophical hermeneutics, the 'narrative turn' in social studies, sociolinguistics and cultural studies.

Hugh MacMahon spent most of his life in Korea and China as a Columban missionary. There he developed a keen interest in East-Asian culture, especially the social influence of Confucianism. He has written a number of books in Korean and English on this East–West encounter, summarizing his experiences in his 2015 book *Guest from the West*. After working with the Irish Missionary Union in Dublin for five years, he now writes on East–West cultural exchange while accompanying Chinese students presently studying in Ireland.

After a long career at University College Dublin (UCD), during which she focused on American and Anglo-Irish literature, **Jerusha McCormack** took early retirement to work as a Visiting Professor at Beijing Foreign Studies University. There she helped found the current Irish Studies Centre while teaching and writing on cultural comparisons between China and the West and, specifically, China and Ireland. Ten years ago, this interest resulted in *China and the Irish* (2009; Mandarin edition, 2010), the first volume of this series, for which her own essay explores the relationship of Oscar Wilde and a fourth-century Chinese sage called Zhuangzi (Chuang Tsŭ). In China, she has lectured not only at Beijing Foreign Studies University but also at Peking University, Fudan, and many other universities throughout the PRC, as well co-teaching an annual comparative course (with John Blair) for the Chinese Studies MPhil at Trinity College Dublin.

Index